SPRING 2015

JANUARY **ROMANS**
FEBRUARY **1 & 2 COR**
MARCH **1 THESS - PHILEMON**
APRIL **1 PETER - JUDE**

OnTrack Devotions: Spring 2015
Published by:
Pilgrimage Educational Resources
1362 Fords Pond Road, Clarks Summit, PA 18411
www.simplyapilgrim.com

For subscription information:
Pilgrimage Educational Resources
1362 Fords Pond Road, Clarks Summit, PA 18411
570.504.1463
ontrackdevotions.com

Printed in the United States of America

Copyright © 2015 Pilgrimage Educational Resources

All rights reserved. No part of this publication may be reproduced, stored in a retrieval system, or transmitted in any form or by any means - for example, electronic, photocopy, recording - without the prior written permission of the publisher. The only exception is brief quotations in printed reviews.

Any internet addresses, email addresses, phone numbers, and physical addresses in this book are accurate at the time of publication. They are provided as a resource. Pilgrimage Educational Resources does not endorse them or vouch for their content or permanence.

Author: Dwight E. Peterson
Executive Developer: Benjamin J. Wilhite
Editor: Kristin Jones
Graphic design by Higher Rock Creative Studio

ISBN-13 978-0692312407
ISBN 0692312404

10 9 8 7 6 5 4 3 2 1

QUICK START GUIDE

Everyone is at a different place in their walk with God and in their Bible study skill. Because of that, OnTrack is designed to engage four progressive user **SKILL LEVELS**. This guide will help you identify your skill level and how to use OnTrack effectively.

IDENTIFY YOUR PERSONAL SKILL LEVEL

Be honest about your own personal level as you begin! Starting beyond your actual level can lead to unnecessary frustration and discouragement. Some level of frustration is good when learning a skill, but too much may tempt you to give up. Pay particular attention to the approach each user should take based on their current SKILL LEVEL.

Level 1: You have spent little or no time in personal Bible study and you have limited knowledge of the Bible. **FOCUS: Key Passage, Devotional Thought.**

Level 2: Most of your experience with the Bible is from church and/or at home. You have been taught from the Bible, but you have not consistently studied it on your own. **FOCUS: Extra Reading, Devotional Thought, answer at least the first two Daily Questions if you can.**

Level 3: You have a bit of experience reading the Bible on your own. Maybe it hasn't always been consistent or you are newer at it, but you are getting comfortable with it. **FOCUS: Extra Reading, Devotional Thought, answer all four Daily Questions.**

Level 4: You have a lot of experience in Bible study and you consistently see solid applications. **Focus: Extra Reading, Devotional Thought, all Daily Questions, and try creating your own questions.**

Every once in awhile, review your current skill level to check whether you should bump it up. You can do this on your own, with an accountability partner, or with a spiritual mentor in your life. Aim to grow!

HOW TO USE ONTRACK

This tool is designed to help you grow your personal Bible study skill as a key part of developing a regular personal conversation with God. You will learn to dig into the text with good questions that lead to understanding and personal life change. To get the most out of OnTrack, follow the progression below:

PRAY. Ask the Holy Spirit to show you exactly what He wants you to see and understand from the Word. If you are in Christ, the Holy Spirit is in you and one of His jobs is to illuminate Scripture for you. He was the person of the Godhead directly engaged in the inspiration of the Word and He knows exactly what He meant when He wrote it.

READ THE WORD. Always start with reading the passage first before reading the devotional thought or any other tools you use to help understand Scripture.

QUICK START GUIDE, CONTINUED

What God has to say is always more important than what anyone else has to say about what God has to say.

READ THE DEVOTIONAL THOUGHT. The purpose of this text is to frame your thinking and to spur good questions, not to tie the passage up with a neat tidy bow.

ANSWER THE QUESTIONS. Some days, the author provides specific questions for you to answer that will help you dig into the text a bit. Other days, you'll see the generic Observation, Interpretation, Application, and Implementation questions. These are days designed to stretch you in the process of creating your own good questions.

ENGAGE OTHERS. One of the key benefits of a tool like OnTrack is that others in your world are working through the same Bible passages every day and engaging the same questions. This provides accountability for you; but more than that, it gives you an opportunity to compare notes and learn with each other. Often, you will see things they did not and vice versa. Bible study can be a team sport! It will help deepen your understanding of Scripture and your relationships.

GET ORIENTED

The following is a quick orientation to a typical OTD day. Use the sample devotional day image on the opposite page for reference.

1. **Header Bar:** It gives you the day of the week, the date, and the key passage for the day. Read the passage in your Bible BEFORE jumping to the next step!
2. **Extra Reading:** This is the complete text for the day. The key passage from the header bar will be in there, but this covers the context of the passage. If you are ready to bite off the whole chunk of Scripture, go for it!
3. **Devotional Thought:** The daily thought is designed to frame your thinking process AFTER you read the verses and BEFORE you answer the questions. It will encourage you to chew on the verses and ponder what God is telling you through His Word. The thought models for you the method of Bible study you are learning for yourself.
4. **Questions:** Each day will have four questions that help you personally work through the process of identifying what God is saying in His Word, then connecting it to your own life. Each question builds on the one before it.

A FINAL NOTE

Be patient and consistent. It's a process. Go at a comfortable pace. Ask God to grow your skill and to give you the discipline to keep at it. It will take time, but if you stick with it, you will be able to study God's Word for yourself.

05.02.13 | THURSDAY

1 SAMUEL 2:1-11

DEVELOPING GODLINESS

SAY WHAT?
(Observation: What do I see?)

SO WHAT?
(Interpretation: What does it mean?)

NOW WHAT?
(Application: How does it apply to me?)

THEN WHAT?
(Implementation: What do I do?)

How do you feel about your relationship with God? Would you like to have more spiritual passion? How would you go about getting it? You could follow the example in this passage. Today we see a woman who had an obvious passion for God. She was excited about her faith and excited about what God was doing in her life. There is an amazing difference between the Hannah of the first chapter and the Hannah in chapter two. What made the difference in her life? It was the difficult circumstances that God had her walk through. Intimacy and passion for God came from the difficult times which drive us to our knees before Him. Without tough times, we never get the deeper walk we desire. God asked Hannah to face some huge challenges. Her willingness to face them and trust God through them caused her to emerge with a greater commitment to God. When God brings these kinds of circumstances into our lives, we need to remember that it is for our good. If we allow it, they will build our character and give us a deeper walk with God. While they may be difficult, they produce Godly qualities.

XTRA READING
1 SAMUEL 2

ONTRACKDEVOTIONS.COM

HELLO
MY NAME IS
SAINT

otrack devotions

2015
JANUARY
ROMANS

MONTHLY PRAYER SHEET

"...The prayer of a righteous man is powerful and effective." James 5:16

Reach out to...	How I will do it...	How it went...

Other requests...	Answered	How it was answered...

MONTHLY COMMITMENT SHEET

Name: _____

This sheet is designed to help you make personal commitments each month that will help you grow in your walk with God. Fill it out by determining
1. What will push you
2. What you think you can achieve

If you need help filling out your commitments, seek out someone you trust who can help you. Share your commitments with those who will help keep you accountable to your personal commitment.

Personal Devotions:
How did I do with my commitment last month? _____
I will commit to read the OnTrack Bible passage and devotional thought _____ day(s) each week this month.

Church Attendance:
How did I do last month with my attendance? _____
I will attend Youth/Growth Group _____ time(s) this month.
I will attend the Sunday AM service _____ time(s) this month.
I will attend the Sunday PM service _____ time(s) this month.
I will attend _____ time(s) this month.
I will attend _____ time(s) this month.

Scripture Memory:
How did I do with Scripture memory last month? _____
I will memorize _____ key verse(s) from the daily OnTrack Devotions this month.

Outreach:
How did I do last month at sharing Christ? _____
I will share Christ with _____ person/people this month.
I will serve my local church this month by _____
_____

Other Activities:
List any other opportunities such as events, prayer group, etc., that you will participate in this month. _____
_____

ONTRACKDEVOTIONS.COM

THURSDAY | 01.01.15

JUST SAYING...   ROMANS 1:1-17

If you were not around and people were talking about you, what would they say? What words would they use to describe you? Would they talk about how committed to Christ you are? Would they say that they respect you? In today's reading, we learn something about the Christians in Rome that hopefully can be said about each of us. Paul wrote to explain the Gospel, the message of Christ. He told them that he had been faithfully praying for them and that he thanked God for them because, their "faith is being reported all over the world." What an incredible statement! When conversation turned to the Christians in Rome, it was about their great faith. In fact, their commitment to Christ was known by people all over the world. It must grieve the heart of God to know that some of us claim to be believers in Jesus Christ, yet not be known at school or work as people who have great faith. It ought to be said of each of us as individuals and corporately as a church, that we are people of great faith. The world ought to be able to know just by observing us that we serve God. Can they see that in your life? What needs to change so they can?

SAY WHAT?
Observation: What do I see?

SO WHAT?
Interpretation: What does it mean?

NOW WHAT?
Application: How does it apply to me?

THEN WHAT?
Implementation: What do I do?

01.02.15 | FRIDAY

ROMANS 1:18-32

GENERAL REVELATION

SAY WHAT?
How do we see God's eternal power in the world?

SO WHAT?
How is God's divine nature seen in the world?

NOW WHAT?
How can you help someone who does not know Christ see God in this world?

THEN WHAT?
In light of this passage, what personal commitment can you make?

According to this passage, what can people conclude about God just by what they generally observe in the world? This section of Scripture reveals two things that can be discovered about God just by observing our world. God has created a world that reveals to everyone, no matter where he lives, that there is a God. In fact, the world reveals to all of us God's invisible qualities. His first invisible quality seen in the world is His eternal power. Mankind can look all around him and see that God is omnipotent. His power is unlimited. Second, the world reveals God's divine nature to mankind. It demonstrates to humanity that God is a God of love and mercy. He cares about us as individuals. And who is able to see these things about God? Everyone! God has not hidden it, but has made it plain to all men. If they miss it, they do so because they have suppressed the truth in their own minds. All will stand before God without excuse, because God has made known to man that He does exist. How we respond to this knowledge determines where we will be spending eternity. How are you responding to what God has revealed?

ONTRACKDEVOTIONS.COM

SATURDAY | 01.03.15

KINDNESS

ROMANS 2:1-16

What attribute of God's character leads people to repentance? We often think that it is His justice or His wrath. We think that God needs to hammer people into repentance. In today's reading, however, we realize it is something different. According to verse 4, it is His kindness. It is incredible to grasp the contrast shown here between God's kindness and man's stubbornness. Paul wrote in the previous chapter that all men stand before God condemned. Man can not save himself and is guilty before God. Although every man deserves hell, God's kindness has provided a way of escape. God sent His Son to the earth that we might find forgiveness of sin. According to Paul, God's riches, tolerance, and patience ought to bring us to repentance. Instead, man responds with stubbornness and with an unrepentant heart. Instead of seeking after God, man is self-seeking and rejects the truth. He, by nature, would rather follow after evil than live by the plan of God. How have you responded to God in your life? How have you responded to His kindness and grace?

SAY WHAT?
Observation: What do I see?

SO WHAT?
Interpretation: What does it mean?

NOW WHAT?
Application: How does it apply to me?

THEN WHAT?
Implementation: What do I do?

01.04.15 | SUNDAY

PROVERBS 16

The book of Proverbs was designed to help us in "attaining wisdom and discipline; in understanding words of insight; in acquiring a disciplined and prudent life, doing what is right and just and fair; in giving prudence to the simple, knowledge and discretion to the young." As you read through this chapter, write down the verses that are most significant to you in your present circumstances.

VERSE | WHAT TRUTH IT COMMUNICATES | HOW IT IMPACTS MY LIFE

MONDAY | 01.05.15

INWARDLY?

ROMANS 2:17-29

How is Paul's message in today's reading true of Christians today? Do you notice any similarities between your church and these Jews? Paul criticized the Jews for an attitude that is not only wrong, but one that could cost them eternity. They thought that because they were Jews by birth, it gave them certain privileges. They were Jews who were familiar with the Law. Therefore, they believed that their knowledge gave them a relationship with God which made them superior to others. They felt that they had the right to instruct others and even guide people in the issues of life. But Paul revealed the error of their attitude. Just because the knowledge they claimed was God's truth, it had not changed their lives. They taught that it was wrong to steal, but they stole. They bragged about their relationship with God, yet dishonored Him with their actions. Christians often have this same attitude. They feel they are superior because they "know" the truth. They talk as if they have a relationship with God, yet live lives no differently than the unbelievers who surround them. Could this describe you? Do you practice what you preach?

SAY WHAT?
In what ways are we like the Jews in today's reading?

SO WHAT?
Why is it so easy for Christians to fall into this trap?

NOW WHAT?
What can you do to prevent this kind of attitude from developing in your own heart or in the hearts of others?

THEN WHAT?
In light of this passage, what personal commitment can you make?

XTRA READING
ROMANS 2 (AGAIN)

01.06.15 | TUESDAY

ROMANS 3:21-31 — FAITH ALONE

SAY WHAT?
Observation: What do I see?

SO WHAT?
Interpretation: What does it mean?

NOW WHAT?
Application: How does it apply to me?

THEN WHAT?
Implementation: What do I do?

If you were to condense the point of today's reading into one sentence, what would it be? Paul is trying to illustrate to us that all men stand before God condemned and can be forgiven only by faith in Jesus Christ alone. The Jews believed that in order to be right with God, one had to observe the Old Testament Law. Paul had to show them that they could not earn their way into heaven, even by observing the Law. Paul demonstrated that the Law only showed people that they stood before God condemned. It was designed to reveal how much they needed a Savior, not to provide them with a means to earn salvation. In verse 28, he said again that one is declared righteous by faith alone and not works. Further, this salvation is available to everyone. Everyone is a sinner, condemned before God, and everyone can find forgiveness through faith in Jesus Christ. You can't attain heaven or a relationship with God by your human effort or your merit, even if your effort contains very good things. Who, in your world, needs to know that he stands before God condemned and that only Christ has provided a way for him to be forgiven? How will you tell him?

XTRA READING — ROMANS 3

ONTRACKDEVOTIONS.COM

WEDNESDAY | 01.07.15

GRACE

ROMANS 4:1-15

Up to this point in his letter, Paul has been working to convince the Romans that salvation is by grace and not by works. How does today's passage support this position? Paul illustrates it by using Abraham, the father of the Jews, and someone about whom they would have knowledge. In Abraham's life, salvation came through grace and not by his works. If salvation came to Abraham by grace, then certainly our salvation would come by grace as well. Paul quoted from the Old Testament in verse 3 to prove this point. He used the Old Testament account to show the readers that Abraham was not even circumcised when God declared him righteous. That alone would demonstrate to the Jews that his works could not have made him righteous, because he was declared righteous before he obeyed the Law. Paul also uses another significant man in Jewish history, David. He illustrates from David's own words that righteousness comes by grace through faith. Realizing that salvation is nothing we can earn, our hearts ought to be filled with humble gratitude to God for all He has done for us. Is yours? Can others tell?

SAY WHAT?
Observation: What do I see?

SO WHAT?
Interpretation: What does it mean?

NOW WHAT?
Application: How does it apply to me?

THEN WHAT?
Implementation: What do I do?

01.08.15 | THURSDAY

ROMANS 4:16-25 — FAITH

How would you describe your faith? On a scale of 1 - 10, 1 being no faith and 10 being never any doubt, how would you rate it? Today, we read an impressive statement about Abraham's faith. Verse 21 tells us that Abraham was "fully persuaded that God had the power to do what He had promised." God said it, and Abraham simply believed God would do what He had said. Abraham was a 10. He did not doubt or wonder if what God said was true. He did not build into his life something to fall back on in case God's plan didn't work out. He just believed God. We can't help but be impressed with a faith that demanded he leave home and go to a land that God would show him, believe God would give him a child in his old age and then be willing to sacrifice his only child. How does your faith compare to Abraham's? It is sobering to realize that without faith, it is impossible to please God. How does your level of faith show up in your daily living? God has never given us any reason to doubt Him. What would it take for you to become a person of faith? What can you do to begin the process as you begin this new year? Find someone who can help you.

SAY WHAT?
In what area of your life is your faith weak?

SO WHAT?
How does the weakness of your faith demonstrate itself?

NOW WHAT?
What can you do to begin growing in your level of faith?

THEN WHAT?
In light of this passage, what personal commitment can you make?

XTRA READING: ROMANS 4 (AGAIN)

FRIDAY | 01.09.15

PERSEVERANCE

ROMANS 5:1-11

Paul tells the Romans in today's reading that they should rejoice in their suffering because it produces perseverance. What about perseverance is so great that these people would rejoice when they had an opportunity to get it? The definition of perseverance is "steadfast endurance, standing our ground, or never giving up." James tells us that, in order for us to be mature and complete, not lacking in anything, perseverance must finish its work. Perseverance is a quality that is necessary to be mature. In this passage, Paul tells us that perseverance produces character, and character produces hope. We can conclude then, that without suffering we have no perseverance, and without perseverance we have no maturity, no character, and no hope. In light of how important perseverance is to our spiritual lives, Paul encourages us to rejoice when suffering comes. It is the only way to acquire perseverance. How are you responding to the suffering that God has allowed in your life? Rejoice, your suffering is producing character that will change your life! Allow it to build perserverance into your life.

SAY WHAT?
Observation: What do I see?

SO WHAT?
Interpretation: What does it mean?

NOW WHAT?
Application: How does it apply to me?

THEN WHAT?
Implementation: What do I do?

XTRA READING
ROMANS 5

01.10.15 | SATURDAY

ROMANS 6:1-14 — KNOW

SAY WHAT?
Observation: What do I see?

SO WHAT?
Interpretation: What does it mean?

NOW WHAT?
Application: How does it apply to me?

THEN WHAT?
Implementation: What do I do?

One of the greatest struggles we have as Christians is gaining victory over sin. In todays and tomorrow's reading, we will learn five keys to gaining victory over sin. Mark them in your Bible. First, Paul says that we must "know" what is true. We must understand and believe what Scripture teaches. It tells us that we were baptized into Christ; therefore, we have new life. We also know that our old self was crucified with Christ. It is dead and has no authority over us. Second, we must "count" ourselves dead to sin. The word count means "letting what you know to be true in your head make its way down to your heart." You believe what Scripture says as truth! Third, "offer" yourselves to God. The progression Paul has in mind is to know the truth, feel it in your gut, and then give yourself to God and not let sin have any control in your life. Yield to God, not to sin. You can say "no" to sin and live a victorious Christian life. We must know the truth, believe the truth, and then live out the truth. Of these three, which one do you need to begin working on? What can you do to start the process? Who can you ask to help you? Living victoriously is possible!

XTRA READING
ROMANS 6

ONTRACKDEVOTIONS.COM

SUNDAY | 01.11.15

PROVERBS 17

The book of Proverbs was designed to help us in "attaining wisdom and discipline; in understanding words of insight; in acquiring a disciplined and prudent life, doing what is right and just and fair; in giving prudence to the simple, knowledge and discretion to the young." As you read through this chapter, write down the verses that are most significant to you in your present circumstances.

VERSE	WHAT TRUTH IT COMMUNICATES	HOW IT IMPACTS MY LIFE

01.12.15 | MONDAY

ROMANS 6:15-23 — A SLAVE

SAY WHAT?
What commands from this chapter do you need to grasp as truth?

SO WHAT?
What can you do for this truth to make its way to your heart?

NOW WHAT?
How can you offer yourself to obedience rather than sin?

THEN WHAT?
How can you serve righteousness as a slave in your day to day living?

In today's reading, Paul gives to us the final ingredients for being able to live a victorious Christian life. If you have not read the first part of the chapter or the devotional thought from Saturday, go back and read it so that you can understand the entire flow of this chapter. The fourth thing we must do to gain victory over sin is to "obey." Sin is not your master and you do not have to obey it. In fact, since you are now a slave to righteousness, having been saved, you must now obey God and not give in to sin. The reality is that you have a choice. You have been set free. You can just say no to sin and yes to righteousness! Fifth, Paul says to "serve" righteousness as if you were a slave. Paul did not say that you will never sin, but that you do not have to sin. We are not helpless against sin's dominance after trusting Christ. Since you have become a slave to righteousness, serve it as a slave. As we have seen from this text, to gain victory one must "know" the truth, "count" himself dead to sin, "offer" himself to God, "obey" what He commands, and "serve" righteousness as a slave. Use today's questions to help you make the changes that will help you to live victoriously.

XTRA READING
ROMANS 6 (AGAIN)

TUESDAY | 01.13.15

OUR NEED

ROMANS 7:7-25

Why did God give the Law to the nation of Israel? What did He want them to see from having it? If we follow what Paul wrote in this chapter without thinking through it, we may come to the conclusion that he thought the Law was a negative thing. Paul anticipated that and addressed it by giving to us four facts concerning the Law. First, he explains that the Law reveals what sin is. Without the Law, we would not know what God considers sin. Second, the Law stirs sin in people. When we know what God expects or what His Law states, our sinful nature desires to disobey it. Third, the Law left man ruined. Man realized that he had no power over sin and gave in to it. Fourth, the Law shows the sinfulness of man. It clearly demonstrates that, without a Savior, man is doomed. There is no way man can overcome sin and fulfill the righteous requirements of the Law without the Savior. Without the Law, we do not see our need and turn to God as the only way of salvation. God desires that we acknowledge who we are and what He's done, but many do not. You cannot live righteously without the Savior. Does your life reflect that truth?

SAY WHAT?
Observation: What do I see?

SO WHAT?
Interpretation: What does it mean?

NOW WHAT?
Application: How does it apply to me?

THEN WHAT?
Implementation: What do I do?

01.14.15 | WEDNESDAY

ROMANS 8:1-17

WHICH ONE?

VERSE:	LIVE BY THE SPIRIT:	THOSE WHO DO NOT:

What happens to those who trust Christ as their Savior? Today's reading gives us the answer to that question. These verses give us a clear contrast of those who live by the Spirit and those who do not. Use the chart provided to record the characteristics of those who live by the Spirit and those who do not. As you do, ask yourself which one describe your life. What you discover will help you know the steps you need to take in order to progress in your walk with God. Be honest as you complete it.

XTRA READING
ROMANS 8

THURSDAY | 01.15.15

FOR GOOD   ROMANS 8:18-39

The substance of what we have learned to this point from reading Romans is incredible. These verses are no different. Paul's letter has demonstrated to us that we can have victory over sin and live a righteous life. Today we see that the process of becoming like Christ is guaranteed! Although it is difficult, and we may wonder at times if we will ever get there, God has guaranteed that it will happen. Paul tells us, in verses 28-30, that God works out "everything" for good. You see, those God saved, He has predestined to be conformed to the likeness of His Son. You and I, who know Jesus Christ as our Savior, will become like Jesus Christ. The events of salvation are not only enough to save us and get us to heaven, but are also enough to make us like Christ. To drive the point home, Paul listed the kinds of things we fear might keep us from becoming like Christ. In verse 37, he stated that we are more than conquerors. He re-emphasized that we will become like Christ. Not only is our salvation guaranteed, but our sanctification is as well. Use these facts to encourage yourself and others to press on. All things work together for good.

SAY WHAT?
Observation: What do I see?

SO WHAT?
Interpretation: What does it mean?

NOW WHAT?
Application: How does it apply to me?

THEN WHAT?
Implementation: What do I do?

01.16.15 | FRIDAY

ROMANS 9:1-18 — FAIR?

SAY WHAT?
Why do you think people have such a hard time understanding election?

SO WHAT?
What impact should this truth have on how we view our own salvation?

NOW WHAT?
How should you respond in light of the fact that God chose you?

THEN WHAT?
What personal commitment should you make in light of what you have read today?

Does God choose some to be saved? According to today's reading, the answer is yes. Does that mean that God chooses some people to go to hell? According to this passage, the answer is no. While this might seem to be a contradiction, this passage helps us understand election more clearly. Paul tells us that men come to Christ according to God's purpose, not because of what they have done. He illustrates this truth with the life of Rebekah. Before the twins, Esau & Jacob, were even born and could do good or evil, God chose Jacob over Esau. Does that make God unjust? No. All men, throughout all time, deserve to go to hell. No one who goes to hell can say he deserved anything else. God has simply chosen to bestow mercy on some. We can accuse God of having selective mercy, but never of being unfair because we all deserve hell. God wants those of us who have received Christ by faith to know we had nothing to do with our salvation. We should have hearts filled with humble gratitude for what God has given to us, and serve Him with love and devotion every day. We have what we don't deserve! Does your life demonstrate that knowledge?

XTRA READING
ROMANS 9

SATURDAY | 01.17.15

PRIDE ROMANS 9:19-33

When the portion of this letter from yesterday was read to the Jews, it must have shocked them. In fact, Paul says as much in verses 30 & 31. How could the Jews, who pursue righteousness with a great deal of effort, miss salvation? Even more astonishing is how could the Gentiles, who did not even pursue righteousness, obtain salvation? The key to understanding this is in the motives of the two groups and their methods of pursuing righteousness. The Jews were trying to obtain righteousness through good works. In their pride, they refused to accept the fact that righteousness was out of their reach. Their pride was so great that instead of allowing the Law to demonstrate that salvation could not be earned, they continued to do good things to earn it. The Gentiles came to God by faith, knowing they could never earn salvation on their own. Pride did not get in the way of their salvation. The Gentiles, in humility, received by faith what the Jews sought after with great effort, but failed to see. Salvation is available to those who realize they could never earn their way into heaven. Are you one of those people? Pride will prevent many from accepting God's gift. Do not let it do that to you!

SAY WHAT?
Observation: What do I see?

SO WHAT?
Interpretation: What does it mean?

NOW WHAT?
Application: How does it apply to me?

THEN WHAT?
Implementation: What do I do?

XTRA READING
ROMANS 9 (AGAIN)

01.18.15 | SUNDAY

PROVERBS 18

The book of Proverbs was designed to help us in "attaining wisdom and discipline; in understanding words of insight; in acquiring a disciplined and prudent life, doing what is right and just and fair; in giving prudence to the simple, knowledge and discretion to the young." As you read through this chapter, write down the verses that are most significant to you in your present circumstances.

VERSE	WHAT TRUTH IT COMMUNICATES	HOW IT IMPACTS MY LIFE

MONDAY | 01.19.15

RESPONSIBILITY
ROMANS 10:1-15

Since God chooses those who are going to be saved, does that mean we do not have to witness to people? Your answer should be absolutely not, unless you failed to read this chapter. While it is true that those who are to be saved will become saved because of what God does, we still must do our part to share the message of Christ with them. We find in these verses two principles that confirm our responsibility. First, in verse 11, we see that everyone who calls on the name of the Lord will be saved. There is no difference between Jew or Gentile. Salvation is available to everyone and we must demonstrate that by sharing the message of the Gospel with all people. Second, verses 14 & 15 clearly state that people will only respond to the message if they first hear it. God has chosen His children to be the means by which the Gospel is communicated. You and I have the awesome responsibility of taking the message to people, so that God can enable them to respond. These verses should motivate us to spread the Gospel to every corner of the world. There are people who are waiting to hear the message. Will you be the one to tell them?

SAY WHAT?
How can you better prepare yourself to share the message of the Gospel with anyone, at any time?

SO WHAT?
How can you maximize your opportunities to share the gospel with people?

NOW WHAT?
Name some friends and family members who need to hear the gospel. How and when will you tell them?

THEN WHAT?
In light of this passage, what personal commitment can you make?

XTRA READING
ROMANS 10

ROMANS 11:1-24 | PROMISES

01.20.15 | TUESDAY

SAY WHAT?
Observation: What do I see?

SO WHAT?
Interpretation: What does it mean?

NOW WHAT?
Application: How does it apply to me?

THEN WHAT?
Implementation: What do I do?

In light of what we have been learning in Romans, are we to conclude that God's promises to Israel have changed? Are those promises transferred to those of us who have accepted Christ? After hearing the letter, some of the Jews must have wondered if the church was going to replace Israel in light of God's promises. Paul clearly states that God has not rejected the Jews or shut them out from salvation. He will keep for Himself a remnant who have accepted Christ, and "will" fulfill the promises He made through these Jews. God is currently allowing Gentiles to be saved and enjoy what He first offered to the Jews. Since many Jews have rejected the Gospel, God has permitted Gentiles the opportunity to be "grafted in." We, who are not Jews, should be humbled to know that we have been given this opportunity to be saved along with the Jews. God is not finished with the Jews, nor has He rejected them. The promises He made to them through Abraham and David will one day be fulfilled. Therefore, we can be sure that the promises He made to us will also be fulfilled, regardless of what the future holds. We will enjoy the blessings of His promises.

XTRA READING
ROMANS 11

WEDNESDAY | 1.21.15
DOXOLOGY
ROMANS 11:25-36

What is a doxology? A doxology is an expression of praise to God. It is the response of a heart filled with the wonder of God. It is often found in Scripture after a description of truth such as we find in today's reading. Paul has written about the wonder of salvation for many chapters. He explained in his letter to the Romans how God made it possible for all to have eternal life and to have their sins forgiven. The more he wrote and described all God did for us, the more praise flowed from his heart. This doxology flows out under the inspiration of the Holy Spirit. As we read it, we can see how Paul viewed his God and the incredible things God has done for him. Have you ever written a doxology? Have you ever been so moved by what you heard or discovered that you wanted to tell God how wonderful He is or how good He has been? Why not take time today to do just that. Think back on what God has been teaching you and write your own doxology. Why not also take some time to share it with a friend?

MY DOXOLOGY

God, you are...

I praise You, for You have...

XTRA READING
ROMANS 11 (AGAIN)

01.22.15 | THURSDAY

ROMANS 12:1-8

TRANSFORMED

SAY WHAT?
Observation: What do I see?

SO WHAT?
Interpretation: What does it mean?

NOW WHAT?
Application: How does it apply to me?

THEN WHAT?
Implementation: What do I do?

Paul makes a major shift in how he has been writing in this chapter. Did you notice it? He started with doctrinal discussions and how we ought to live in light of the truth he has described. Now, he writes about practical ways these truths ought to impact our lives. One of those ways is to not allow ourselves to be conformed to the world. How do we keep ourselves from being conformed to the world? The answer to that question is simple. It is just hard to accomplish. In order to keep ourselves from being conformed to the world, we must be transformed. According to verse 2, we are transformed by renewing our minds. This is the key to keeping ourselves from being conformed to the world. We renew our minds by saturating it daily with Scripture. We renew our minds by memorizing Scripture so that we can recall it when we need to. We renew our minds by refusing to allow the pollution of the world to enter it. Renewing our minds means being careful what we allow our eyes to see. It is simple, but hard. Be aware of what you knowingly and unknowingly allow in your mind. Be committed to the renewing of your mind.

XTRA READING
ROMANS 12

FRIDAY | 01.23.15

LOW POSITION   ROMANS 12:9-21

If we looked at the people you spend your time with, what would we discover? What does the spiritual condition of the people you spend most of your time with tell us about yours? What does their popularity tell us about you? What does how popular the people I hang around with have to do with who I am? According to today's reading, the answer to all those questions is a lot! Paul gives us instructions about dealing with people. He talks about those who persecute you and those who are your enemies. Then, in verse 16, he makes an important statement. He says, "be willing to associate with people of low position." Paul realized that pride will keep you from doing just that. If you hang around only with the popular or beautiful people, then you are proud. Paul would tell us to stop being proud and be willing to spend time with people of low position. Invite them to go with you to a party. Ask them to sit with you at church. Choose them for your study group. In other words, be their friend. The question still remains - what do the people you spend your time with tell you about yourself? When is the last time you associated or identified with people of low position?

SAY WHAT?
How can you better "associate" with people of low position?

SO WHAT?
Why is it that you do not do this more often?

NOW WHAT?
What needs to change in your life for you to fulfill God's expectations in this area?

THEN WHAT?
In light of this passage, what personal commitment can you make?

ROMANS 13:8-14

01.24.15 | SATURDAY
13:14 PRINCIPLE

SAY WHAT?
Observation: What do I see?

SO WHAT?
Interpretation: What does it mean?

NOW WHAT?
Application: How does it apply to me?

THEN WHAT?
Implementation: What do I do?

What do you think about during the day? If we could play a video of your thoughts today, would you be comfortable if anyone saw it? In today's reading, we have one of the most important principles in the Bible that helps us with our battle against sin. It is found in verse 14. In fact, you could call it the 13:14 principle. In this verse, Paul tells us to clothe ourselves with the Lord Jesus Christ and to not even think about how to gratify the desires of our sinful nature. It goes beyond the act of sin, to actually keeping us from thinking of ways to entertain or contemplate sin. The implication here is that when we channel surf and pass a station and we know something sinful is about to come on, we do not "accidentally" pass that channel again, but skip it altogether. When we could mistakenly see something in a store or hear something if we linger, we move away so that we do not. It is making our priority the prevention of any impure sight or sound from entering our minds. We do not put ourselves in a position where we can sin. We guard our minds and allow no thought to enter that dishonors God. How are you doing with the 13:14 principle?

XTRA READING
ROMANS 13

SUNDAY | 01.25.15

PROVERBS 19

The book of Proverbs was designed to help us in "attaining wisdom and discipline; in understanding words of insight; in acquiring a disciplined and prudent life, doing what is right and just and fair; in giving prudence to the simple, knowledge and discretion to the young." As you read through this chapter, write down the verses that are most significant to you in your present circumstances.

VERSE	WHAT TRUTH IT COMMUNICATES	HOW IT IMPACTS MY LIFE

01.26.15 | MONDAY

ROMANS 14:1-12 — DECISIONS

SAY WHAT?
Observation: What do I see?

SO WHAT?
Interpretation: What does it mean?

NOW WHAT?
Application: How does it apply to me?

THEN WHAT?
Implementation: What do I do?

When you are faced with an important decision, how do you decide what to do? If you find yourself in a situation which requires a decision, you will find great encouragement from today's reading. Paul tells us that when we need to make choices in our lives, we need to keep two important thoughts in mind. First, our motives need to be pure and our lives lived unto the Lord. Our desire ought to be to please Him and bring glory to His name, not what appears to be the most comfortable or easiest for us. Secondly, we must keep in mind that we will all appear before the judgment seat to give an account for the choices we have made. It is not others who evaluate the choices we make, it is God Himself who will evaluate each of our choices. With these two thoughts in mind, how do the choices you have made measure up? Have you thought about what others are doing and what they might think as opposed to what God thinks? Remember, do everything as unto the Lord, and never forget it is before Him you will stand to give an account. Those two thoughts will guide you to make right decisions.

XTRA READING
ROMANS 14

TUESDAY | 01.27.15

STUMBLING
ROMANS 14:13-23

Today, we find an important principle regarding how we ought to respond to our brothers and sisters in Christ. It is one that is often misunderstood. Paul tells us that, in light of what he previously wrote, we are to stop judging and make up our minds to not put a stumbling block or obstacle in our brother's way. What implications does that have? It means that we are not to engage in any activity that would result in a weaker brother being led into sin. We should carefully consider what we do in light of what a young Christian would think. We may tempt him to sin. How would we do this? Many times a weaker brother evaluates right or wrong based on our choices. Some things which may be fine for us may not be for someone else. Our behavior could influence him in negative way. Soon he may be making unwise decisions in light of his background or where he is in his walk with God. Some may also stumble when our actions violate their consciences. If you engage in an activity which makes a friend uncomfortable, do you justify your actions, belittle him, or rather do something else? Our choices should always be regulated by their impact on others. Are yours?

SAY WHAT?
Observation: What do I see?

SO WHAT?
Interpretation: What does it mean?

NOW WHAT?
Application: How does it apply to me?

THEN WHAT?
Implementation: What do I do?

XTRA READING
ROMANS 14 (AGAIN)

01.28.15 | WEDNESDAY

ROMANS 15:1-13
SCRIPTURE

What impact does Scripture have on you? Make a list of some of the ways it has changed you recently. An important way Scripture ought to influence you is found in verse 4 of today's reading. Did you notice it? One reason God deals with the many topics, issues, and expectations in Scripture is to encourage us and increase our endurance. As we read and spend time in it, Scripture enables us to endure painful circumstances. It provides the strength to keep pressing on. People who spend little or no time in the Scripture are people who are more prone to quit or give up under pressure. What is the result of spending time in Scripture? We have HOPE! God wants to give us hope, and He gives it through His Word. When we feel like giving up, we need to go to the Word. When we are discouraged, we need to go to the Word and in it find endurance and encouragement. As a result, God will flood our hearts with hope. Often, when we are discouraged or feel like giving up, Scripture is the last place we go. Make the reading of God's Word THE priority of your life. Contained in the pages is everything you need. With every need, open the Word. Don't go a day without reading God's Word.

SAY WHAT?
In what ways has Scripture changed your life?

SO WHAT?
What passages have you read recently that have given you hope?

NOW WHAT?
What have you read recently that has helped you endure a difficult situation?

THEN WHAT?
What personal commitment can you make about your Bible reading?

XTRA READING
ROMANS 15

THURSDAY | 01.29.15
CHARACTERISTICS
ROMANS 15:14-33

If a friend of yours was asked to list three characteristics that you're known for, which ones would they choose? Hopefully, the traits would be the three that Paul used in today's reading to describe the Romans. First, he said that they were full of goodness. They were morally right and were known for their virtue. Would people describe you in this way? Second, they were complete in knowledge. That did not mean that they had arrived and knew everything about the Bible, but that they were doctrinally sound. They must have spent time in the Word and paid attention to solid Bible teaching. Would people say you are complete in knowledge? Third, they were competent to instruct. The word used here for instruct is most often translated admonish. It is not teaching or leading a Bible study, but giving counsel, encouragement, warning, or a rebuke to people. Are you competent to instruct others? Is your lifestyle and level of Biblical knowledge such that you could encourage or counsel others? What would it take for you to become someone who is known by these characteristics? When will you get started?

SAY WHAT?
What would you need to change to become someone known for being full of goodness?

SO WHAT?
What would it take for you to be known for being complete in knowledge?

NOW WHAT?
What would it take for you to be competent to instruct?

THEN WHAT?
In light of this passage, what personal commitment can you make?

01.30.15 | FRIDAY

ROMANS 16:17-27

INFLUENCER

SAY WHAT?
Observation: What do I see?

SO WHAT?
Interpretation: What does it mean?

NOW WHAT?
Application: How does it apply to me?

THEN WHAT?
Implementation: What do I do?

Think through the past few years and name the people who have been an influence in your life. Have you let them know how much you appreciated it? In this chapter, Paul did just that. He closed his letter by naming individuals who had encouraged and influenced his life. How encouraging it must have been for Phoebe to know that she had touched the life of Paul and had her name written in this letter. When the letter was read publicly, those whose names were mentioned must have really been blessed and encouraged. Too often, we do not take the time to let people know the affect they have had on our lives. In fact, the people who have touched our lives the most probably do not even know they have done so. Why not take some time today to tell someone you know how much you appreciate them and the influence they have had on your life. It would encourage them so much. Why not also think of ways you can become a person who is touching the lives of others more often? What would it take to become someone who would get the kind of note we are talking about?

XTRA READING
ROMANS 16

SATURDAY | 01.31.15

EVALUATION

PSALM 139:23-24

You are now one month into the new year. How are you doing? Are you making progress on the goals you set back in December? Those spiritual disciplines you determined to develop, are you developing them? The people you wanted to impact for Christ, are you building those relationships? Why not take some time today for some self examination? You may have entered this year with some goals to see yourself change in some areas and grow in others. Ask God to clearly reveal to you areas in which you need to make adjustments. Use the questions and today's Bible reading to help. Be honest and willing to make the changes necessary.

SAY WHAT?
What were some of my goals for 2015?

SO WHAT?
What progress am I making in those areas?

NOW WHAT?
What adjustments do I need to make based on my observations?

THEN WHAT?
How am I going to make sure those adjustments take place?

the fire will test what sort of work each one has done.

— 1 Corinthians 3:13

OnTrackDevotions.com

MONTHLY PRAYER SHEET

"...The prayer of a righteous man is powerful and effective." James 5:16

Reach out to...	How I will do it...	How it went...

Other requests...	Answered	How it was answered...

MONTHLY COMMITMENT SHEET

Name: _____

This sheet is designed to help you make personal commitments each month that will help you grow in your walk with God. Fill it out by determining
1. What will push you
2. What you think you can achieve

If you need help filling out your commitments, seek out someone you trust who can help you. Share your commitments with those who will help keep you accountable to your personal commitment.

Personal Devotions:
How did I do with my commitment last month? _____
I will commit to read the OnTrack Bible passage and devotional thought _____ day(s) each week this month.

Church Attendance:
How did I do last month with my attendance? _____
I will attend Youth/Growth Group _____ time(s) this month.
I will attend the Sunday AM service _____ time(s) this month.
I will attend the Sunday PM service _____ time(s) this month.
I will attend _____ time(s) this month.
I will attend _____ time(s) this month.

Scripture Memory:
How did I do with Scripture memory last month? _____
I will memorize _____ key verse(s) from the daily OnTrack Devotions this month.

Outreach:
How did I do last month at sharing Christ? _____
I will share Christ with _____ person/people this month.
I will serve my local church this month by _____
_____

Other Activities:
List any other opportunities such as events, prayer group, etc., that you will participate in this month. _____
_____

SUNDAY | 02.01.15

PROVERBS 20

The book of Proverbs was designed to help us in "attaining wisdom and discipline; in understanding words of insight; in acquiring a disciplined and prudent life, doing what is right and just and fair; in giving prudence to the simple, knowledge and discretion to the young." As you read through this chapter, write down the verses that are most significant to you in your present circumstances.

VERSE	WHAT TRUTH IT COMMUNICATES	HOW IT IMPACTS MY LIFE

02.02.15 | MONDAY

1 CORINTHIANS 1:18-31

AVAILABILITY

SAY WHAT?
Observation: What do I see?

SO WHAT?
Interpretation: What does it mean?

NOW WHAT?
Application: How does it apply to me?

THEN WHAT?
Implementation: What do I do?

What does it take to be someone whom God can use? How smart would you need to be? How popular do you need to be? What kind of talent would be necessary? Paul gives us the answer to those questions in today's reading. According to Paul, it only takes being "foolish," "weak," "lowly," and "despised." I think most of us will find ourselves in at least one of those categories. You see, according to verse 29, God chooses these kinds of people so that no one can boast about themselves. If God used only the "great" people, then the watching world would not see the power of God. They would think the results were because of the abilities of the people involved. God desires to show His great power to the world through you. It is not your ability that determines if God can use you. He is interested in your availability. Have you allowed Him to use you? He has "enriched you in every way," according to verse 5; therefore, allow Him to use you today. Do not look at your own abilities, but look at God's capabilities to use you in the lives of others. You will be amazed at what He can do through you! Why not allow Him to start today!

XTRA READING
1 CORINTHIANS 1

ONTRACKDEVOTIONS.COM

TUESDAY | 02.03.15

SO THAT

1 CORINTHIANS 2:1-5

Reread the first five verses of this chapter and, at the end of each verse, ask yourself the question "Why?" One would think that Paul would want to use eloquent speech and superior wisdom when he spoke to people about Christ. One would think that he would want his message to contain wise and persuasive words so the listeners would respond to what he was saying. Why didn't he use them? He did not want people to respond to the message of Christ because of his abilities or methods. He wanted them to respond because the Spirit of God was moving in their hearts. Paul wanted people to respond to the message of salvation because of a demonstration of the Spirit's power. Otherwise, they would be deceived into believing something supernatural had happened. Over time, they would fall away. In what way can the Holy Spirit's power be demonstrated by us? Our transformed lives is one way! If we needed great wisdom, eloquence, or persuasive words, some of us wouldn't be very effective. However, each of us ought to have a transformed life that can be seen by others. Is your life demonstrating the Spirit's power to those who are watching?

SAY WHAT?
Observation: What do I see?

SO WHAT?
Interpretation: What does it mean?

NOW WHAT?
Application: How does it apply to me?

THEN WHAT?
Implementation: What do I do?

XTRA READING
1 CORINTHIANS 2

02.04.15 | WEDNESDAY

1 CORINTHIANS 3:1-9 — DIFFERENT ROLES

SAY WHAT?
In what ways can God use you to "plant" a seed?

SO WHAT?
In what ways can God use you to "water" a seed?

NOW WHAT?
What is an example from your life in which you did the planting or watering but God used someone else to make it grow?

THEN WHAT?
In light of this passage, what personal commitment can you make?

There is an encouraging phrase in today's reading. Did you notice it? This book was written to a church that had several problems. From this chapter we learn that there was jealousy and quarreling among them. One of the issues was a dispute over Paul and Apollos. Some felt superior because they had been saved through Paul's ministry, while those who had been saved through Apollos' felt they were superior. To counter the jealousy, Paul gave them principles to guide them. One of the principles is found in verse 8, in the phrase, "according to his own labor." This phrase teaches us that the results of someone's ministry, or his impact on others lives, is in God's hands alone. He alone determines the results in the lives of people. You may have planted the seed while someone else watered it. Later, someone else came along and harvested it. We must be willing to play the role God has designed and trust Him with the outcome. What role might God want you to be playing in people's lives right now? Are you ready to plant, water or harvest? What is keeping you from doing that today? Use today's questions to help you get started.

XTRA READING
1 CORINTHIANS 3

ONTRACKDEVOTIONS.COM

THURSDAY | 02.05.15

CONSISTENT

1 CORINTHIANS 4:14-21

If you want to know what made Paul such an effective witness, you need to look no further than today's reading. It is what also gave him the ability to confront the Corinthian church with the issues in this book. What is it? You'll find it if you look in verse 17. Paul says that he has a life that "agrees with what I teach everywhere in every church." What a statement! No wonder he had such power. He was a person in whom there was no hypocrisy and could, therefore, make such a statement. What he preached and taught to others was what he lived. He did not address other's issues knowing his life had areas that had not been made right. Nor did he have to avoid saying what needed to be said because his own life did not measure up. His life was consistent with what he said and taught. When you put the truth of God together with a consistent life, you have incredible power. Could you make this statement? Does your life agree with "everything" you say? Our world desperately needs to see people living a life consistent with what they claim to believe. What area do you need to work on so this can be true of you? Who can you ask to help you become more consistent?

SAY WHAT?
Observation: What do I see?

SO WHAT?
Interpretation: What does it mean?

NOW WHAT?
Application: How does it apply to me?

THEN WHAT?
Implementation: What do I do?

XTRA READING
1 CORINTHIANS 4

02.06.15 | FRIDAY

1 CORINTHIANS 5:1-8

DEAL WITH IT

SAY WHAT?
Observation: What do I see?

SO WHAT?
Interpretation: What does it mean?

NOW WHAT?
Application: How does it apply to me?

THEN WHAT?
Implementation: What do I do?

Today's reading reveals another problem facing the church in Corinth. They had sin in their church and, not only were they not dealing with it, but they were proud that they were tolerant of people and had not been judgmental. They patted themselves on the back as though it was to their credit that the guilty party felt no shame. They felt ignoring his sin was better than dealing with it out in the open. Paul explained why this response is wrong. First, the Corinthians response to sin did not help the person come to see his sin as wrong before God. By not confronting it, they led him to believe he was fine and his sin was not a problem. Secondly, their response was wrong because it would allow sin to spread throughout the church. Others would assume that they could engage in this kind of behavior also. Sin in our churches cannot be tolerated or ignored. We must lovingly confront it and, if there is no repentance, we must take a stand for the sake of the one sinning, as well as for the church. It may not be easy, but it must be done. There is too much at stake! Is there sin in your life you have not dealt with? Is there sin in your church?

XTRA READING
1 CORINTHIANS 5

SATURDAY | 02.07.15

BENEFICIAL

1 CORINTHIANS 6:12-20

When we are confronted with a choice in an area of our lives that Scripture does not cover, how do we know what choice to make? How do we know what God would have us do? In today's reading, Paul gives us two principles to consider when confronted with that kind of situation. First, verse 2 says you need to ask yourself if this is something that is beneficial for you spiritually. That is, will it help you become more like Christ, and will it help you reach your world for Christ? The question to ask is not "Will this hurt me?" but "How will this help me?" A second question to ask yourself is whether it will cause you to become controlled by it through addiction or habit. Drugs and alcohol are obvious examples. They are wrong because they become my master and control my behavior. There are many areas these principles govern that we need to examine. Ask yourself not only if the activity is permissible, but if it is beneficial and if it will enslave you. In what areas of your life do you need to be asking these questions? What area is the Spirit of God confronting you with as you read this? What will you do about it?

SAY WHAT?
What kinds of things might be okay, but would not be "beneficial" for you?

SO WHAT?
What kinds of things might be okay but could control you?

NOW WHAT?
What specific area of your life do you need to examine with these two questions in mind?

THEN WHAT?
What personal commitment can you make in light of this passage?

XTRA READING
1 CORINTHIANS 6

1 CORINTHIANS 7:17-24

02.08.15 | SUNDAY

STAYING PUT

SAY WHAT?
Observation: What do I see?

SO WHAT?
Interpretation: What does it mean?

NOW WHAT?
Application: How does it apply to me?

THEN WHAT?
Implementation: What do I do?

Paul gives a common theme in verses 17, 20, 24, and 26. Did you pick up on it when you read through these verses? What is it? How does it apply to our lives right now? Often, when we make spiritual decisions, we think it means we need to make major, sweeping changes. That may be true sometimes, but there are some areas that should not change. In the Corinthian church, they thought getting saved meant finding a new wife if you were married to an unbeliever. If a slave trusted Christ, he might think that his decision meant his standing needed to change. Paul explained that you can be a Christian and live for God while remaining in your present circumstance. If God called you to be a slave, be the best slave you can possibly be. If you are married to an unsaved spouse, then seek to honor God in your marriage. Often, we are exactly where God wants us to be, but are prone to jump ship or bail out. Paul discouraged that kind of attitude. Our spiritual decision might open doors to reach those in our world. In what present circumstance do you need renewed determination to hang on and allow God to work? God has you there for a reason.

XTRA READING
1 CORINTHIANS 7

ONTRACKDEVOTIONS.COM

MONDAY | 02.09.15

BUT LOVE... **1 CORINTHIANS 8:1-13**

When addressing eating meat sacrificed to idols, why did Paul begin with verses 1-3? Why talk about how knowledge puffs people up? Why emphasize how important love is? Paul began here so this church would realize immediately that it is possible to pursue knowledge and only gain pride. Knowledge alone will not keep you from doing something that may hurt a brother, even though your action may not be wrong. Love, on the other hand, does not lead to pride, but humility. Its goal is to build others up, not hurt people. If someone were only interested in knowledge, he wouldn't care if eating meat hurt someone else. All he would care about is the question of right and wrong. He would work to simply gain more knowledge about the matter. Paul wanted the Corinthian church to have their knowledge affected by love. If it is, it will be motivated by what is best for others, not what is best for me. Because Paul was motivated by love, he could say what he did in verse 13. Can you? Are there things you will not give up, even though they may hurt another brother? If you are motivated by love, you will seek to benefit others.

SAY WHAT?
Observation: What do I see?

SO WHAT?
Interpretation: What does it mean?

NOW WHAT?
Application: How does it apply to me?

THEN WHAT?
Implementation: What do I do?

Xtra Reading
1 CORINTHIANS 8-9

02.10.15 | TUESDAY

1 CORINTHIANS 10:23-33

WHATEVER

SAY WHAT?
In what small, insignificant areas of your life can you glorify God?

SO WHAT?
How will you go about accomplishing that task?

NOW WHAT?
How can you remind yourself what this passage teaches throughout the day?

THEN WHAT?
What personal commitment can you make in light of this passage?

Why does Paul use the illustration of eating and drinking to challenge those in Corinth to glorify God? It would seem that eating and drinking are the most insignificant things we do in the course of a day. Surely he could come up with a more significant illustration. Illustrations like what career we choose or how we use our money might attract our attention better. But that may be his point. Paul clearly states that "everything" we do ought to glorify God. Even in the areas of our life which seem routine and insignificant, we ought to seek to bring Him glory. His point is that we should glorify God not just when we stand before people in a public way, but when we mow the lawn, wait in line, or hang out with our brothers and sisters - in "everything." He used an insignificant example to illustrate how important glorifying God is in every area of our lives. In what "small" area of your life do you need to seek to glorify God? Choose one area and begin today. Circle the words "eating" and "drinking" to remind you of what this passage teaches. Your life is on display. You may never realize what those around you have observed.

XTRA READING
1 CORINTHIANS 10

ONTRACKDEVOTIONS.COM

WEDNESDAY | 02.11.15

COMMUNION | 1 CORINTHIANS 11:17-34

How serious is the communion service to God? Are our actions during communion important? Is God even aware that it takes place? When you read this chapter, you will realize communion is very important to God-probably more important than you thought. Paul included this chapter because the Corinthians were struggling with how they conducted communion. They came to the service with great division among themselves. Some did not wait, but began eating on their own, some excluded individuals, and others were even getting drunk during the service. Paul made it very clear how significant communion is to God and that it should not be taken lightly. Some of the members of their church were sick and had even died because they did not respond in a right way to this service of celebration. Communion is a solemn time to reflect on what Christ did for us at Calvary. It is also a time for us to examine our lives for sin and where we are in our relationship with God. Do you take time to reflect on what Christ went through for you? Do you think about how your life has changed? Remember how significant this service really is the next time you attend.

SAY WHAT?
Observation: What do I see?

SO WHAT?
Interpretation: What does it mean?

NOW WHAT?
Application: How does it apply to me?

THEN WHAT?
Implementation: What do I do?

XTRA READING
1 CORINTHIANS 11

02.12.15 | THURSDAY

1 CORINTHIANS 12:12-31 — UNITY BY DESIGN

What causes dissension in a local church? How can we prevent it? In today's reading, Paul condemns two responses believers have that destroy unity. Could you be guilty of one of these responses? Paul begins this chapter by writing that everyone has at least one gift that God has given him to be beneficial to the entire body. How do you respond to this information? One way is to look at yourself and determine that you are insignificant because you are not like others, and your gift is not one of the "important" ones. That response is wrong and hurts the unity of the body. A second response would be to examine others and determine that they are not important because they are not like you or do not have what you consider to be "important" gifts. This response is also wrong and hurts unity. We must all realize that God has given to each of us, all the members of the body of Christ, gifts to use in the church. If we take ourselves out or push others out, we hurt the body. We also miss out on what those gifts are designed to give. Have you struggled with either of these responses? Are you using the gifts God has given you? Do you see the role others must play in the body?

SAY WHAT?
What kind of gifts could make a person feel unimportant to the body?

SO WHAT?
In what ways do we make people feel like they are not important to the body?

NOW WHAT?
Look again at #1 and list a way that God can use those gifts to impact the body.

THEN WHAT?
What personal commitment can you make in light of this passage?

XTRA READING
1 CORINTHIANS 12

FRIDAY | 02.13.15

LOVE

1 CORINTHIANS 13:1-13

Why would Paul follow up a discussion about spiritual gifts with a section on love? One might assume that he would follow the last chapter with a discussion on how to use different spiritual gifts. Or maybe a discussion on how to determine what spiritual gift you have. Could it be that Paul follows his discussion on gifts with love because love is the most important quality a church could have? We could assume that if a church had a great preacher it would be a great church. But Paul says that without love, it would sound awful. We could assume that if your church had great spiritual power, enough faith to move mountains, it would be a great church. But without love, it would be a church that amounts to nothing. We could assume that if your church made great sacrifices in order to meet the needs of the poor, or was willing to suffer personal harm, it would be a great church. But without love, all these sacrifices gain nothing. Paul followed his discussion of the gifts with love, the most important ingredient for a church. Without love, no matter what spiritual gifts your church might have, it will amount to nothing. Without it, nothing else matters.

SAY WHAT?
Observation: What do I see?

SO WHAT?
Interpretation: What does it mean?

NOW WHAT?
Application: How does it apply to me?

THEN WHAT?
Implementation: What do I do?

XTRA READING
1 CORINTHIANS 12-13

02.14.15 | SATURDAY

1 CORINTHIANS 14:13-25

GUIDELINES

SAY WHAT?
Observation: What do I see?

SO WHAT?
Interpretation: What does it mean?

NOW WHAT?
Application: How does it apply to me?

THEN WHAT?
Implementation: What do I do?

What if the members of a local body use their gifts but are not motivated by love? In this chapter, we see the consequences in a church that used their spiritual gifts, but was not motivated by love. You may see your own church fitting this description. As the believers in Corinth used their gifts, pride and jealousy developed among them. These divisive elements resulted from misuse of gifts and self-edification, rather than building the body. They concluded that one's spiritual gift determined how spiritual he was. In their minds, the use of certain gifts demonstrated that they were more spiritual than someone who had a different gift. To make matters worse, people at church were using their gifts in a way that was causing confusion, and the worship of God was being hindered. Paul gives some very specific and direct guidelines to avoid these problems continuing. The key was that they were using their gifts in a way that was not pleasing to God. Love was not the motivation of their lives, but pride. Do you see similar characteristics in your church? How are you using the gifts God has given to you? What can you do to avoid these abuses in your life and in your church?

XTRA READING
1 CORINTHIANS 14

SUNDAY | 02.15.15

RESURRECTION

1 CORINTHIANS 15:12-34

In today's reading, we find one of the greatest chapters in the Bible on the Resurrection of Christ. There is so much in these verses that we could write many different insights or thoughts. However, rather than look at what we might pull out of this passage, think about how this chapter speaks to you. The following questions will help you walk through these verses and highlight what you find there. Take the time to read it and respond to the questions. It could change your life forever!

SAY WHAT?
What facts about the Resurrection did you learn from reading this chapter?

SO WHAT?
Why is the Resurrection important to Christians?

NOW WHAT?
What would the implications be if Jesus did not rise from the dead?

THEN WHAT?
According to verse 58, what ought your response be?

XTRA READING
1 CORINTHIANS 15

02.16.15 | MONDAY
1 CORINTHIANS 16:1-4 — GIVING

SAY WHAT?
Observation: What do I see?

SO WHAT?
Interpretation: What does it mean?

NOW WHAT?
Application: How does it apply to me?

THEN WHAT?
Implementation: What do I do?

What standard does God have for giving to the church? When does He expect me to give? How can I, as a teenager or an adult, know if God is pleased with what I am putting in the offering plate each Sunday? These questions are not only important today, they were issues at the church in Corinth, and Paul closes his letter by addressing them. First, he gives instruction that people were to give every week- not once a month, not every other week. How often do you put money in the offering plate at your church? Second, what was the standard for how much they were to give? According to Paul, it was dependent upon their income. Everyone is expected to give, and the amount they give is determined by their income. God knows how much you make, and He expects you to give accordingly. How do you do with these instructions? It is shameful that we are often not taught that God has expectations for giving for everyone. When was the last time you took a portion of what you made from babysitting or your job and put it in the offering plate at church? This week would be a good time to get started.

XTRA READING
1 CORINTHIANS 16

ONTRACKDEVOTIONS.COM

TUESDAY | 02.17.15

WHY?

2 CORINTHIANS 1:1-11

Why do bad things happen to God's people? If you have ever asked that question, you will find some of the answers in today's reading. In this section of Scripture, Paul gives us two reasons why bad things happen to God's people. The first reason is found in verse 4. Bad things happen to God's people so that they will be able to more effectively reach out and comfort those who are going through a similar difficulty. We are able to give them hope by sharing with them how God comforted us in the midst of our trouble. We would have empty words if only the unsaved experienced trouble and God's people never did. A second reason that bad things happen to God's people is so they will learn to rely on God, not themselves. The greater the trial, the greater the need to depend on God. When things are going well, we often forget about God and try to handle everything on our own. Sometimes good things cause us more trouble than bad things. In difficult times, remember that God has a purpose. Seek to allow His purpose to be accomplished in your life. What purpose could there be for your present trouble? How should you respond to what God has allowed?

SAY WHAT?
Observation: What do I see?

SO WHAT?
Interpretation: What does it mean?

NOW WHAT?
Application: How does it apply to me?

THEN WHAT?
Implementation: What do I do?

XTRA READING
2 CORINTHIANS 1

02.18.15 | WEDNESDAY

2 CORINTHIANS 2:5-11

NOW...

SAY WHAT?
What can you do to communicate to someone that you forgive them?

SO WHAT?
How can you comfort someone whom you have forgiven?

NOW WHAT?
How can you reaffirm your love for someone you have forgiven?

THEN WHAT?
What personal commitment can you make in light of what this passage teaches?

To understand this chapter, you need to remember the instructions Paul gave to the Corinthians concerning the man who was living in sin in 1 Corinthians 5. You may want to go back and read it again. Understanding the context will enable you to more fully understand its message. When the church received the instructions from Paul in chapter 5 of 1 Corinthians, they followed them. Because they did, the man who was in sin repented. The problem here was that they would not forgive him. Paul gave instructions on what to do after someone has repented of his sin. First, they must forgive him (2:7). Secondly, after forgiving him, they need to comfort him (2:7). Repentance is followed by sorrow for sin and sometimes it is overwhelming. Finally, they are to reaffirm their love for him (2:8). Those who do not respond to a repentant sinner in this way are committing sin. Circle the words "forgive," "comfort," and "reaffirm," to remind yourself of how you need to respond to those seeking forgiveness. Could there be someone in your life who has sinned and repented, but you have not forgiven? How can you follow these steps?

XTRA READING
2 CORINTHIANS 2

THURSDAY | 02.19.15

PROCESS

2 CORINTHIANS 3:7-18

What does the verb "being" communicate to you? Does it communicate to you a process, or a moment in time? Why even ask the question? Because Paul uses this verb to illustrate something very important to us. It is a crucial factor of the Christian life. Believers often see the Christian life as something that takes place in a moment in time. A decision was made at camp or at a church service and the expectation is to be completely different immediately. We can become discouraged when change hasn't taken place overnight and can cause us to doubt the sincerity of the decision. In verse 18, Paul states that we are "being" transformed into the likeness of Christ. He uses this word to illustrate that our growth is a process. Becoming like Christ does not happen in a moment in time. The key is to look for growth. Am I more like Christ this year than last year? The actual decision is needed to begin the process and make change possible. However, change takes place over a period of time. What steps do you need to take in order to move forward in your Christian life? Circle the word "being" in your Bible to remind you it's a process.

SAY WHAT?
Observation: What do I see?

SO WHAT?
Interpretation: What does it mean?

NOW WHAT?
Application: How does it apply to me?

THEN WHAT?
Implementation: What do I do?

XTRA READING
2 CORINTHIANS 3

02.20.15 | FRIDAY

2 CORINTHIANS 4:7-18 — LIGHT & MOMENTARY

SAY WHAT?
What troubles have you have faced in your life?

SO WHAT?
What positive results have come in your life because of these troubles?

NOW WHAT?
How can God use these troubles to help others in your future?

THEN WHAT?
What personal commitment can you make in light of what this passage teaches?

What two adjectives did Paul use to describe his troubles in verse 17? Circle them in your Bible. Are they the same two words you would use to describe the troubles you are facing right now or have faced in the past? Paul used them because of how he viewed troubles. He knew that though outwardly he was being "pounded on," inwardly God was doing a great work in his heart. God was renewing him and comforting him in the midst of his trials. Paul knew that the troubles he faced were accomplishing something very important in his life. In light of his perspective, he did not lose heart when trials came his way. When he looked at eternity and what God was accomplishing in his life, his troubles seemed "light" and "momentary." Maybe you need to begin today by fixing your eyes not on what you can see - your problems - but on what you can't see - God's work in your heart. Maybe you need to focus on what God is accomplishing in your life as Paul does in this passage. To help, make a list of positive results that have come from the troubles you have experienced in the past. Use the questions to help you focus on what God is doing in your life.

XTRA READING
2 CORINTHIANS 4

SATURDAY | 02.21.15

GUARANTEE
2 CORINTHIANS 5:1-10

If the Holy Spirit was given to "guarantee" our salvation, does that mean I can live however I want and still go to heaven? Not according to what Paul says in this chapter. Paul tells us what our response ought to be to the truth that the Holy Spirit is a deposit guaranteeing our salvation. First, this truth ought to result in living a life of confidence in our salvation, knowing we have eternal life. We should never doubt our salvation or wonder if a sin we committed would result in losing it. Our salvation is guaranteed. Second, notice what that confidence produces. It produces motivation to please God no matter where we are (2:9). The fact that our salvation is guaranteed does not mean we can do whatever we want, it means we desire to do whatever God wants us to do. Why? Because one day we will all appear before the judgment seat of Christ. You see, eternal security is not a license to do whatever you want and still go to heaven, it is the motivation to serve and please God at all times. If eternal security has not motivated you in this way, as it should, maybe you don't understand what it really means. How should this affect your life and how you live it?

SAY WHAT?
Observation: What do I see?

SO WHAT?
Interpretation: What does it mean?

NOW WHAT?
Application: How does it apply to me?

THEN WHAT?
Implementation: What do I do?

XTRA READING
2 CORINTHIANS 5

02.22.15 | SUNDAY

2 CORINTHIANS 6:14-18 — DATING

SAY WHAT?
Observation: What do I see?

SO WHAT?
Interpretation: What does it mean?

NOW WHAT?
Application: How does it apply to me?

THEN WHAT?
Implementation: What do I do?

Can a saved person marry an unsaved person and it not be considered sin? From today's reading, you realize that the answer is no. But does this passage speak to the issue of dating unsaved people? It does, if you understand the principles involved here. Look closely at what it says. Paul gives us the reasons why God forbids a believer from being yoked together with an unbeliever in marriage and in other relationships. He says it is because we have nothing in common (vs14). We can't have real fellowship (vs14), we find no harmony (vs15), and we find no agreement with the unsaved (vs16). In other words, all that is involved in a good dating relationship could not be possible between a saved person and an unsaved person. How can we enjoy dating someone with whom we have nothing in common, no real fellowship, no harmony, and no possibility of agreement? While this passage does not say that dating the unsaved is wrong, it gives solid reasons to discourage it. We need to love, reach out, and seek to win the unsaved. However, using a dating relationship to win the lost can be confusing and dangerous.

XTRA READING
2 CORINTHIANS 6

MONDAY | 02.23.15

TRUE REPENTANCE

2 CORINTHIANS 7:2-13

How can you tell if someone is demonstrating true godly sorrow over his sin? How do you know if he is truly repentant or just acting as if he is sorry. Paul lists some defining characteristics of godly sorrow in this chapter. We can use these to examine our own life and others' lives in the matter of repentance. Paul heard how this church responded to the correction he wrote in his first letter to the Corinthians. He knew they had genuine, godly sorrow because they had demonstrated 7 characteristics which he listed in verses 10-11. You should number them in your Bible. First he saw that they had an earnestness and an eagerness to clear themselves and to make it right. Second, he saw indignation and alarm about what they had done. They felt terrible about their sin. Third, he saw that they had a longing, a concern, and a readiness to see justice done. They were prepared to accept the consequences their sin required. Does your life reflect these characteristics when you sin against God? Have you seen it in the lives of others? If not, ask God to show you or them the true nature of sin, so that godly sorrow might lead to true repentance.

SAY WHAT?
How might someone who has an earnestness and eagerness to clear himself act?

SO WHAT?
How might someone who has indignation and alarm about what he has done act?

NOW WHAT?
How might someone who has a longing, a concern, and a readiness to see justice done in response to his sin act?

THEN WHAT?
What personal commitment can you make in light of what this passage teaches?

XTRA READING
2 CORINTHIANS 7

02.24.15 | TUESDAY

2 CORINTHIANS 8:1-15 — GIVING

SAY WHAT?
Observation: What do I see?

SO WHAT?
Interpretation: What does it mean?

NOW WHAT?
Application: How does it apply to me?

THEN WHAT?
Implementation: What do I do?

What is your church known for? If we talked to people in your town and asked them what they knew of your youth group or church, what would they tell us? Would they describe it the way the church in Macedonia is described in this passage? Wouldn't it be exciting to be part of a church that has such a heart for giving? To be described in this way is a great honor. So many people see Christians as selfish and uncaring. How important is it to be a giving church? In verse 7 of chapter 8, Paul gives 5 areas in which the church at Corinth excelled. They excelled in faith, speech, love, knowledge, and complete earnestness. Paul also wanted them to excel in their giving. It is wonderful to be a church that is known for the five things Paul listed. But a church also needs to be a giving people in order to be all that God wants it to be. What words would you use to describe your church? What words would you use to describe yourself? Do you give out of your poverty with "extreme generosity" and then give even beyond your ability? In what ways can you improve in this area and also help your church to improve in its giving? How will you begin?

XTRA READING
2 CORINTHIANS 8-9

ONTRACKDEVOTIONS.COM

WEDNESDAY | 02.25.15

NOT WISE — 2 CORINTHIANS 10:7-18

When you read verses 12-18, did they encourage you or concern you? Does this standard reveal that you are doing okay or that you are not where you need to be? For some, it is very encouraging to know that our standard is not based on other people. We can become discouraged by comparing ourselves to others and realize that we can't be what they are or what they think we should be. How comforting to know that God is the only one we need to please. Others, however, compare themselves to those around them and feel fine with where they are in their walks with God. We may not be where we should be spiritually, but compared to some, we are fine. This passage should concern you if you are one of those people who determines you are fine compared to those around you. To compare ourselves to any standard but God's is, as Paul says, "not wise." Comparisons either discourage you from service and joy, or fill you with misplaced confidence in where you stand. Using this as your guide, how do you stand in your walk with God? Determine today to stop comparing yourself to others and use God's standard. He alone is who we must please.

SAY WHAT?
Observation: What do I see?

SO WHAT?
Interpretation: What does it mean?

NOW WHAT?
Application: How does it apply to me?

THEN WHAT?
Implementation: What do I do?

XTRA READING
2 CORINTHIANS 10

2 CORINTHIANS 11:1-15

DECEPTION

02.26.15 | THURSDAY

SAY WHAT?
In what ways does Satan deceive people into viewing God as restrictive?

SO WHAT?
In what ways does Satan deceive people into believing that God's motives are anything but love?

NOW WHAT?
What Scripture verses can you memorize to quote when Satan uses these methods against you?

THEN WHAT?
What personal commitment can you make in light of what this passage teaches?

How did the serpent deceive Eve in the garden? Why not go back to Genesis 3 and read the account again to refresh your memory? If you look closely at Genesis 3, you will see Satan used a method which is still being successfully used today. It is also a method Paul was afraid Satan would use on those in the church at Corinth. First, in Genesis 3, you see that Satan tried to get Eve to see God as being restrictive. Instead of Eve looking at all the other trees in the garden she could eat from, her attention was drawn to the one tree from which God told her not to eat. Then, Satan got her to question God's motives for His instructions and expectations. Satan implied God had given instructions, not for her good or because He loved her, but because He was unkind and selfish. Has Satan tried to convince you that God's ways are restrictive and unfair? Do you focus on what you do not have rather than on all He has given you? Has he tried to convince you that God does not have your best interest at heart and is unkind and selfish? If so, memorize Scripture so that you can quote it when Satan tries to deceive you. Resist him, and he will flee.

XTRA READING
2 CORINTHIANS 11

FRIDAY | 02.27.15

BUT...

2 CORINTHIANS 12:1-10

When trouble comes your way, how do you respond? When you are not getting the playing time you want on your athletic team, how do you respond? When someone at work or school is really getting on you, how do you respond? Do you try to unburden yourself of the situation or complain about it? When someone gets an award or promotion you deserved, how do you respond? Maybe you should rejoice. If you come to view troubles the way Paul did in this chapter, you will. Paul had something in his life that was a great struggle for him. Some feel it was a physical illness; others think it was a person or people who opposed him. Whatever his "thorn in the flesh" was, he did not like it and wanted God to take it away. However, God showed him that He would not remove it because God wanted to take what Satan meant for harm and use it for Paul's good. God did, however, tell Paul He would give him the grace to respond to his thorn in a way that would allow God's power to rest on him. When Paul saw that, he rejoiced. From the list of examples Paul gives in verse 10, which one do you need to see as a gift from God to make you strong? Ask God to help you see trouble as Paul did.

SAY WHAT?
Observation: What do I see?

SO WHAT?
Interpretation: What does it mean?

NOW WHAT?
Application: How does it apply to me?

THEN WHAT?
Implementation: What do I do?

XTRA READING
2 CORINTHIANS 12

02.28.15 | SATURDAY

2 CORINTHIANS 13:1-10

PERFECTION?

SAY WHAT?
Observation: What do I see?

SO WHAT?
Interpretation: What does it mean?

NOW WHAT?
Application: How does it apply to me?

THEN WHAT?
Implementation: What do I do?

Why did Paul close this book by admonishing those in Corinth to aim for perfection? That seems like an impossible goal and one that would discourage the church. Why not just tell them to do the best they could and remember they are human and God understands when they fail? Most likely, Paul closed with that admonition so they did not become satisfied with the progress they were making in their walks with God and with what was happening in the church. Paul didn't want the changes they were making to stop until they had reached perfection. He did not want them to be satisfied with where they were personally or where the group was until they became, personally and as a church, perfect. So, he gave them this goal to shoot for. What is it that you shoot for? Though you may have experienced great growth in your personal life, don't become satisfied. Aim for perfection. Even though your youth group or church is growing and God is at work, don't become satisfied; aim for perfection. Make it your goal, and seek every day to become everything God wants you to be. Make up a small sign to put in your house, school, or workplace to remind you of this goal.

XTRA READING
2 CORINTHIANS 13

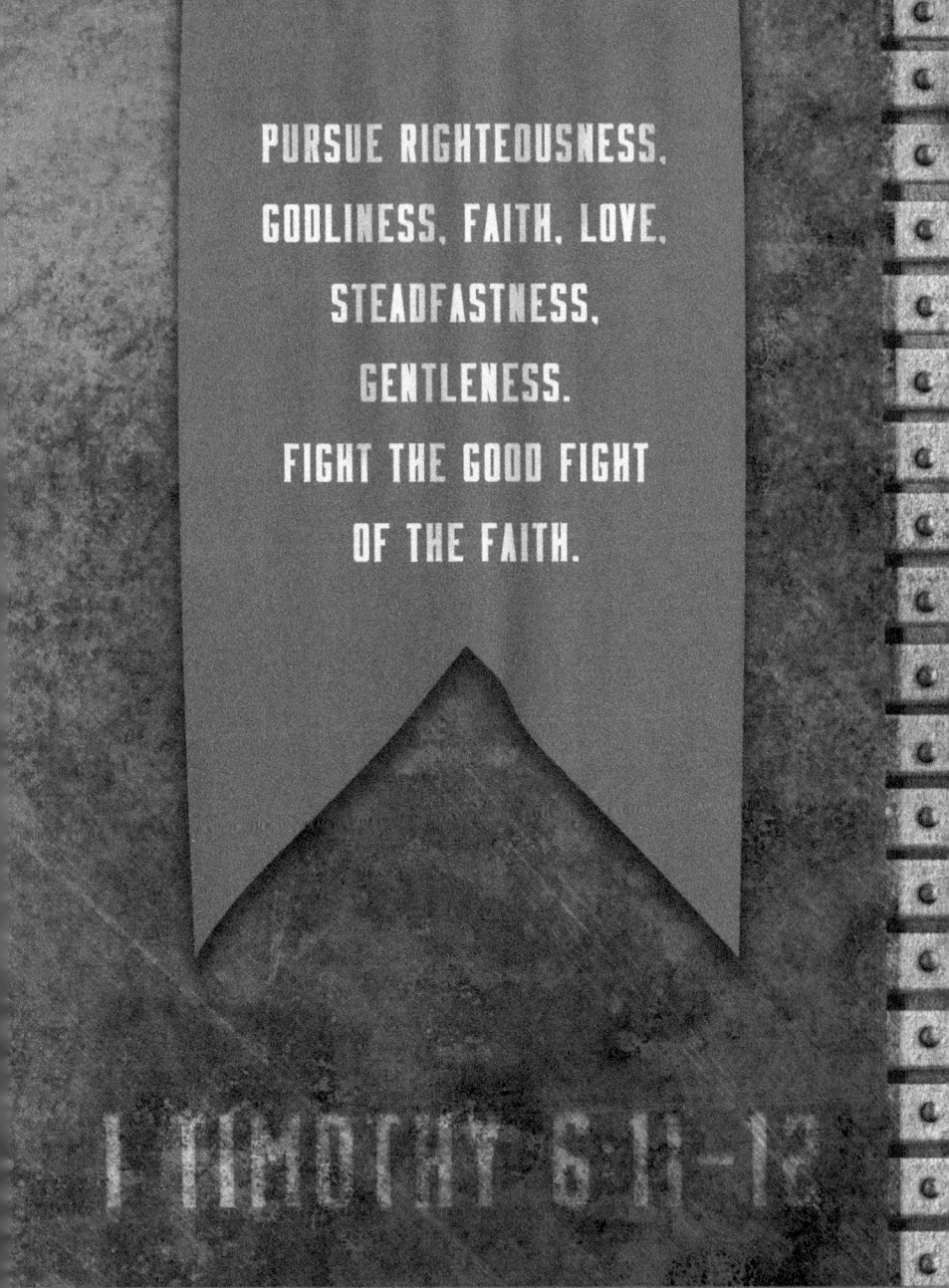

MONTHLY PRAYER SHEET

"...The prayer of a righteous man is powerful and effective." James 5:16

Reach out to...	How I will do it...	How it went...

Other requests...	Answered	How it was answered...

MONTHLY COMMITMENT SHEET

Name: _____

This sheet is designed to help you make personal commitments each month that will help you grow in your walk with God. Fill it out by determining
   1. What will push you
   2. What you think you can achieve

If you need help filling out your commitments, seek out someone you trust who can help you. Share your commitments with those who will help keep you accountable to your personal commitment.

Personal Devotions:
How did I do with my commitment last month? _____
I will commit to read the OnTrack Bible passage and devotional thought _____ day(s) each week this month.

Church Attendance:
How did I do last month with my attendance? _____
I will attend Youth/Growth Group _____ time(s) this month.
I will attend the Sunday AM service _____ time(s) this month.
I will attend the Sunday PM service _____ time(s) this month.
I will attend _____ time(s) this month.
I will attend _____ time(s) this month.

Scripture Memory:
How did I do with Scripture memory last month? _____
I will memorize _____ key verse(s) from the daily OnTrack Devotions this month.

Outreach:
How did I do last month at sharing Christ? _____
I will share Christ with _____ person/people this month.
I will serve my local church this month by _____
_____

Other Activities:
List any other opportunities such as events, prayer group, etc., that you will participate in this month. _____
_____

SUNDAY | 03.01.15

PROVERBS 21

The book of Proverbs was designed to help us in "attaining wisdom and discipline; in understanding words of insight; in acquiring a disciplined and prudent life, doing what is right and just and fair; in giving prudence to the simple, knowledge and discretion to the young." As you read through this chapter, write down the verses that are most significant to you in your present circumstances.

VERSE	WHAT TRUTH IT COMMUNICATES	HOW IT IMPACTS MY LIFE

03.02.15 | MONDAY

1 THESSALONIANS 1:6-10 — EVIDENCE

SAY WHAT?
In what ways do you imitate Christ?

SO WHAT?
What attitude do you display toward the Word of God when you read or hear it?

NOW WHAT?
What comments would people make regarding your character?

THEN WHAT?
How has your life changed since you trusted Christ?

How do you know if true conversion has taken place in the life of someone with whom you have shared Christ? How can you tell if it is really a work of God or if he is simply responding to the way you presented the Gospel? Paul helps us answer these questions in today's reading. He begins this book with the realization that this church responded to the power of the Holy Spirit, not to his words. He knows they are truly saved because he saw four characteristics in their lives. First, he saw that they were becoming imitators of Christ and were a people who walked with God. Second, they received the Word of God with joy and excitement. They wanted to attend church to learn what Scripture teaches. Third, their faith had become obvious to others due to the change in their lives. Fourth, they had given up their former way of life and began serving God. Paul used their daily lives as a measuring stick to determine whether or not they had turned to the true God. What changes have taken place in your life that demonstrate to others that God has worked? Do you see the characteristics Paul describes? How can you see them to an even greater degree?

XTRA READING
1 THESSALONIANS 1

ONTRACKDEVOTIONS.COM

TUESDAY | 03.03.15

SUCCESS

1 THESSALONIANS 2:1-12

Why was Paul's ministry so successful? What can we learn from him in this passage that will ensure success in our ministries? There are some important reasons why Paul did not fail, in spite of incredible obstacles. Reasons which, when applied to our lives, will also yield fruit. First, Paul had the right motives (vs3-6). He was not performing to please people. He was serving God because he wanted to please the God Who had given him a message to proclaim. Second, he used the right method (vs7-9). He not only worked at communicating the truth of God's Word, but he had also opened up his life to those he was teaching. He didn't just preach to them, he got involved in their lives and they in his. Third, he had the right message (vs10-12). He taught them to live lives worthy of God. At times, his message was to encourage, comfort, or urge, but always to enable them to walk worthy before God. How successful are you at influencing your world for Christ? Take some time today to examine yourself in these three areas. What is your motive, method and message? In what ways do you need to change?

SAY WHAT?
Observation: What do I see?

SO WHAT?
Interpretation: What does it mean?

NOW WHAT?
Application: How does it apply to me?

THEN WHAT?
Implementation: What do I do?

XTRA READING
1 THESSALONIANS 2

03.04.15 | WEDNESDAY

1 THESSALONIANS 2:17-3:5

LOVE FOR PEOPLE

SAY WHAT?
In what ways do you demonstrate this kind of love for people?

SO WHAT?
In what ways can you improve your love for people?

NOW WHAT?
What steps can you take to begin improving in this area?

THEN WHAT?
In light of this passage, what personal commitment can you make?

On a scale of 1 - 10, how would you rate your love for people? If 10 was a perfect Christlike love for people and 1 was no love for people at all, where would you place yourself? How does your rating compare to the love Paul demonstrated in today's passage? He told the Thessalonians that he longed to see them and be with them. When he was apart from them, he missed them. Do you love people in this way? He wanted to encourage them in their faith. His desire was to help them move forward in their walks with God. Do you love people this way? He continually thought about them and was concerned that they might be tempted and led astray. He was filled with a desire to keep them from falling. Do you have this kind of concern for the people in your world? When he heard about their growth and how faithful they were in their walks with God, he rejoiced. To know that they were growing gave him joy even in the midst of personal difficulty. Often, we live day to day concerned about ourselves only and unwilling to care about others. Look at Paul's example and compare it to your life. What conclusions do you come to?

XTRA READING
1 THESS 2-3

THURSDAY | 03.05.15

MORE & MORE

1 THESSALONIANS 4:1-12

How do you feel about where you are spiritually right now? What words would you use to describe your walk with God? Have you seen growth over the past few months? In what specific areas have you seen it? Today, Paul reminds us of the need to keep growing in our relationship with God and not be satisfied with where we are. In verse 1, Paul wrote that he knew the Thessalonians were living a life that pleased God. Keep in mind that this wasn't their opinion of themselves, it was the Apostle Paul's opinion. We can assume from this that their lives did please God. Notice though, what he wrote next. He told them to continue, "more and more." Even though they were living godly lives, Paul encouraged them to work harder at it. Likewise you should not be satisfied with living the life you now live, even if it is pleasing to God. Make it even more pleasing to God. Paul then listed areas in which they could improve. In order to please God more, it is necessary that we all examine our lives and improve in areas that are lacking. You may be living a life that pleases God right now, but there is always room to improve.

SAY WHAT?
Observation: What do I see?

SO WHAT?
Interpretation: What does it mean?

NOW WHAT?
Application: How does it apply to me?

THEN WHAT?
Implementation: What do I do?

XTRA READING
1 THESSALONIANS 4

03.06.15 | FRIDAY

1 THESSALONIANS 4:13-18

RAPTURE

SAY WHAT?
Observation: What do I see?

SO WHAT?
Interpretation: What does it mean?

NOW WHAT?
Application: How does it apply to me?

THEN WHAT?
Implementation: What do I do?

What facts about the rapture of the church does this section of Scripture teach us? If we look closely, we are given several. Number them in your Bible. First, we are assured that since Jesus has risen from the dead, those who have died in Him will also rise (vs14-15). People who have trusted Christ before death will be raised again when Christ returns at the rapture. Second, we learn the sequence of the events (vs16-17). Christ will come down from heaven with a shout and with a trumpet call of God. Then, those who were saved before they died will rise from their graves. Finally, those who are alive will meet them and together go up to meet the Lord in the air. Third, we learn that after the rapture we will never again be separated from Christ (vs17). Fourth, we learn that the dates and times of His coming are not known by any man. And lastly, we learn that, since we do not know when the rapture will take place, we need to be ready for it to come at any time. Are you? If Jesus comes today, would the people you influence be ready? There is an eternal price to pay for those who aren't.

XTRA READING
1 THESS 4 (AGAIN)

SATURDAY | 03.07.15

ALWAYS?

1 THESSALONIANS 5:12-28

Of all the final instructions in today's reading, which one affects you the most? Which one is the most difficult for you to obey? How about being joyful ALWAYS and giving thanks in ALL circumstances? Paul gave the Thessalonians (and us) a command that is extremely difficult to obey. It would have been easier had he used the words, "most of the time." One of the most common reasons for not obeying that command is that we do not often see our circumstances the way God sees them. We often forget that God is in control and He has an important purpose for what He does through our circumstances. He may be preparing us for something in the future. He may be giving us an opportunity to grow in an area of blindness. He may be providing us an opportunity to demonstrate to our world the difference He makes in our lives. When we rejoice and are joyful, we show that we believe what God has said. Are you facing a difficult circumstance that is robbing you of joy? What circumstances do you find yourself facing that make it hard to give thanks? What might God be trying to accomplish through them?

SAY WHAT?
Is there a situation that is robbing you of joy and thanksgiving?

SO WHAT?
List a few reasons that you can give thanks in the midst of it.

NOW WHAT?
What can be done to help you follow God's expectations in this area?

THEN WHAT?
In light of this passage, what personal commitment can you make?

XTRA READING
1 THESSALONIANS 5

03.08.15 | SUNDAY

PROVERBS 22

The book of Proverbs was designed to help us in "attaining wisdom and discipline; in understanding words of insight; in acquiring a disciplined and prudent life, doing what is right and just and fair; in giving prudence to the simple, knowledge and discretion to the young." As you read through this chapter, write down the verses that are most significant to you in your present circumstances.

VERSE	WHAT TRUTH IT COMMUNICATES	HOW IT IMPACTS MY LIFE

MONDAY | 03.09.15

GROWTH

2 THESSALONIANS 1:1-4

If your friends were to talk about your life, what would they say? Would hearing what they say encourage or discourage you? Could they say what Paul said about the Thessalonians in this first chapter? Paul first mentioned that he had noticed their faith was growing more and more. Is your faith stronger today than it was 6 months ago? Paul could see that their love for each other was also growing. Can you point to signs that show your love for others has also grown? Finally, Paul said that they were demonstrating perseverance and faith in the midst of persecution and trials. They hung in there and did not give up even when the going got tough. As you look back over the past months, do you think this could be said about you? Have you demonstrated perseverance and faith in the midst of persecution and trials? It is discouraging to be someone who cannot see signs that growth is taking place. Is your faith and your love for others the same as it was 6 months ago? Are you strong enough to persevere in hard times? What needs to change so you can see more growth?

SAY WHAT?
What part of your life demonstrates that your faith is growing?

SO WHAT?
What qualities demonstrate that your love for others is growing?

NOW WHAT?
What in your life demonstrates that you have perseverance and faith in persecution and trials?

THEN WHAT?
In light of this passage, what personal commitment can you make?

XTRA READING
2 THESSALONIANS 1

03.10.15 | TUESDAY

2 THESSALONIANS 2:1-12 — OPPORTUNITY

SAY WHAT?
Observation: What do I see?

SO WHAT?
Interpretation: What does it mean?

NOW WHAT?
Application: How does it apply to me?

THEN WHAT?
Implementation: What do I do?

If you heard the Gospel, rejected it, and therefore missed the rapture, is it possible to be saved during the Tribulation? Today's reading gives us helpful information to answer this frequently asked question. First, Paul tells us that the Holy Spirit will be taken away during the Tribulation. His influence of holding back sin will no longer be a part of this world (vs7). Second, we learn that, during the Tribulation, Satan will perform counterfeit miracles, signs, and wonders in an effort to deceive people (vs9). These efforts will cause people to believe that he, not Jesus Christ, is the Messiah. Third, we learn that God allows a powerful delusion to deceive people so that they believe the lie. Whatever Satan will tell them about the events going on at this time they will believe. God will allow people who have rejected Christ to believe the lie of Satan. They will be condemned and will not become believers. This passage would seem to indicate that those who have rejected Christ before the rapture will not accept Him during the Tribulation. To reject Christ is a very serious decision. One can't assume he will have an opportunity later.

XTRA READING
2 THESSALONIANS 2

WEDNESDAY | 03.11.15

IDLE 2 THESSALONIANS 3:6-15

What does the word "idle" mean in this passage? Why could Paul speak so strongly about idleness in today's reading? He was able to speak against idleness so strongly because he probably wasn't an idle man. How are we to respond to idle people? The word translated here is a military term which means "out of rank." It is a Christian who is acting "out of rank." In the context of this passage, Paul was referring to the specific behavior of not working for a living. It means being lazy or unwilling to work. No one could ever say that about Paul. He knew that, as a believer, he should be the hardest of workers. He knew that being lazy and unwilling to work hard indicated a serious spiritual problem. We often see teens and adults today who are unwilling to work hard for anything. People can be lazy and seem to work harder getting out of work than they would by just doing the job. Idleness characterizes every area from athletics and academics, to employment and helping out at home. God expects Christians to be the hardest of workers, not idlers. To be idle is to sin against God. How do you measure up to God's standard? Make an honest evaluation.

SAY WHAT?
Observation: What do I see?

SO WHAT?
Interpretation: What does it mean?

NOW WHAT?
Application: How does it apply to me?

THEN WHAT?
Implementation: What do I do?

XTRA READING
2 THESSALONIANS 3

03.12.15 | THURSDAY

1 TIMOTHY 1:1-11 **LOVE**

SAY WHAT?
Is your heart pure? What changes are necessary for you to have greater love?

SO WHAT?
Is your conscience good? What changes are necessary for you to have greater love?

NOW WHAT?
Is your faith sincere? What changes are necessary for you to have greater love?

THEN WHAT?
In light of this passage, what personal commitment can you make?

Where does a heart of love come from? If you want to have a heart of love, what should you do? You could turn to today's reading and find out. This passage gives us a way to examine ourselves to be able to tell if our love is not what it ought to be. Mark these qualities in your Bible. In verse 5, Paul says that love comes from having a pure heart, a good conscience, and a sincere faith. First, a pure heart is one that is without sin and is wholly devoted to Christ. Is your heart pure? If you have sin in your life, or if other things are more important than God, you can't love as you should. Second, Paul says that love comes from a good conscience. It is a conscience that works correctly. It does not bother you because your relationships are right and your sin is confessed. If your conscience is not good, you cannot have love. Third, Paul says that love comes from a sincere faith. It is a faith that has no hypocrisy. If you live a hypocritical life, you cannot love. How are you doing in these three areas? You can't have a heart of love without being successful in these areas. Use today's questions to examine your life and determine if you have real love.

XTRA READING
1 TIMOTHY 1

ONTRACKDEVOTIONS.COM

FRIDAY | 03.13.15

SO THAT....   1 TIMOTHY 1:12-20

Can you and I guarantee that we will fulfill the purpose God has for our lives? Is there a way to know for sure that we will not ruin our lives or fail to accomplish what God has for us? The answer is yes according to today's reading. In verse 18, Paul gave Timothy two instructions that would enable him to fulfill the prophecies made about him. First, Timothy had to hold on to faith. That is, he needed to remain loyal and committed to the revealed truth of God found in the Scriptures. Unlike those who had fallen away, Timothy was instructed to remain devoted to the Scriptures. He had to study, guard, defend, know, and apply it to his life. Second, if Timothy were going to stay the course, he had to hold on to a good conscience. That was only possible if he lived a pure life. If he allowed sin to enter his heart, he would fall away and fail to fulfill God's call on his life. Though it is by no means easy, staying true in our walks with God is simple. We must stay true to the Word. We must know it, follow it and share it. We must maintain a good conscience. We cannot tolerate any sin in our lives. Making sure you are faithful to your daily Bible reading is one way to make sure these two happen!

SAY WHAT?
Observation: What do I see?

SO WHAT?
Interpretation: What does it mean?

NOW WHAT?
Application: How does it apply to me?

THEN WHAT?
Implementation: What do I do?

XTRA READING
1 TIMOTHY 1 (AGAIN)

03.14.15 | SATURDAY

1 TIMOTHY 2:1-7 — UNSAVED

SAY WHAT?
Observation: What do I see?

SO WHAT?
Interpretation: What does it mean?

NOW WHAT?
Application: How does it apply to me?

THEN WHAT?
Implementation: What do I do?

How often do you pray for the unsaved? How often does your church pray for unsaved people? When we understand this chapter, we will understand the expectations on our prayer lives, individually and corporately. In today's reading, Paul makes it clear that we as Christians ought to make prayer for the unsaved a very high priority. Paul used the words "first of all" in verse 1 to indicate this. He gave several reasons in this section to pray for the unsaved. First, praying for the unsaved is the right thing to do. Second, God desires for all to come to the knowledge of the truth and be saved. Third, we should pray for the unsaved because it is consistent with what God has called us to do. The reason we are still here on the earth is to be able to reach the world with the message of Christ. There is only one way to receive salvation, and it is our responsibility to share this message. It is clear from this passage that we, as individuals and as specific groups of believers, ought to be praying for the unsaved. If you are not praying like this, why not begin now? Ask God to give you a burden for the lost and a desire to share.

XTRA READING
1 TIMOTHY 2

SUNDAY | 03.15.15

PROVERBS 23

The book of Proverbs was designed to help us in "attaining wisdom and discipline; in understanding words of insight; in acquiring a disciplined and prudent life, doing what is right and just and fair; in giving prudence to the simple, knowledge and discretion to the young." As you read through this chapter, write down the verses that are most significant to you in your present circumstances.

VERSE	WHAT TRUTH IT COMMUNICATES	HOW IT IMPACTS MY LIFE

03.16.15 | MONDAY
1 TIMOTHY 3:1-13 — PASTORS

SAY WHAT?
Observation: What do I see?

SO WHAT?
Interpretation: What does it mean?

NOW WHAT?
Application: How does it apply to me?

THEN WHAT?
Implementation: What do I do?

What do we learn about pastors in today's reading? There is much beyond the specific list of qualifications. First, we learn that it is a very important calling. It is not something to be entered into lightly. Second, we learn that it is a limited calling. Becoming a pastor is not for everyone. It is limited in that it is not for women or for all men. Only a select few are qualified. Third, we learn it is a compelling calling. It is a calling that comes from God and results in an inner passion of the one called. Fourth, it is a responsible calling. It comes with great responsibility and a very high standard. Fifth, it is an honorable calling. It is the highest quality and most important work one could do. Finally, it is a demanding calling. It takes a lot of effort and some plain, hard work. It is not something you can do half-heartedly. It is no wonder Paul lists the character qualities required for a man called to be a pastor. The position of a pastor is to be taken very seriously. The pastorate is not for everyone. It is for those whom God has chosen. Could God be calling you into full-time ministry as a pastor? How will you know? Are you ready?

XTRA READING: 1 TIMOTHY 3

TUESDAY | 03.17.15

NEGLECT
1 TIMOTHY 4:6-16

How could someone neglect his gift? What would one have to do in order for this to be true of him? It must have been an important issue because Paul included this admonition in his charge to Timothy in this chapter. Timothy was told many things that are obviously important. But why did he mention neglecting his gift? Paul knew that even someone like Timothy could fall into the trap of neglecting the gifts God had given him. How? He could neglect them by not using them. He could try to do things only utilizing the human strength God had given him. He could even overlook his gifts by being distracted into doing something other than what God wanted. Timothy could neglect them by falling into sin, and not be able to use them as God had intended. He could neglect his gifts by desiring a different one. He could neglect his gifts by determining to use it to minister in his own way, not the way God intended. Neglecting his gifts would hinder or even kill his ministry. Could you be neglecting the gifts God has given to you in any of these ways? What gifts has God given you? How are you using them? Is it the way God intends for you to use them?

SAY WHAT?
What gifts do you think God has given to you?

SO WHAT?
When people talk about the way you influence their lives, what do they say?

NOW WHAT?
What can you do to make sure you do not neglect the gifts God has given to you?

THEN WHAT?
In light of this passage, what personal commitment can you make?

XTRA READING
1 TIMOTHY 4

03.18.15 | WEDNESDAY

1 TIMOTHY 5:1-16 — PARENTS

SAY WHAT?
Observation: What do I see?

SO WHAT?
Interpretation: What does it mean?

NOW WHAT?
Application: How does it apply to me?

THEN WHAT?
Implementation: What do I do?

As your parents get older, whose responsibility is it to care for them? The answer is found in today's reading, and it might surprise you. Paul, in today's reading, gives Timothy some very clear instruction regarding specific groups of people. In verse 3, he explains to Timothy that he, as a pastor, is to instruct family members to take care of their mother if she becomes widowed. Her children and grandchildren have the responsibility to care for their mother and grandmother if she has lost her husband. The reason for this responsibility is found in verse 4. It is a way of repaying her for the care she gave to her children while they were growing up. Paul makes it clear that when we leave home, we do not leave responsibilities to our parents behind. As our parents grow older, it becomes our responsibility to care for them as it was theirs to care for us when we were unable to care for ourselves. To neglect this responsibility is to disobey God. As you grow older, do not forget God's expectations when the time comes to care for your parents. It will be your opportunity to acknowledge the sacrifices they made and the times they were inconvenienced for you while under their care.

XTRA READING: 1 TIMOTHY 5

ONTRACKDEVOTIONS.COM

THURSDAY | 03.19.15

MASTERS

1 TIMOTHY 6:1-2

How do you respond to those in authority over you? What if that person is harsh or cruel? What if he makes a decision that is unfair? What if he is a Christian? Paul tells us how we ought to answer those questions at the end of this passage. He instructs Timothy to teach his flock that they should treat their masters as people who are worthy of full respect. The reason? - So that God's name and the message of the Gospel would not be slandered. Those watching their lives would notice the difference and would form opinions about Christ based on the actions of the believers. He also explains that those who have fellow believers as masters are not to treat them with less respect. It appears that the Ephesians felt that if their masters were believers, they did not have to give them the same respect as unbelievers. Paul corrects that thinking. He wants the believing masters to be treated better than unsaved masters. How do you respond to those who have authority over you who are saved? Does your behavior and testimony encourage them, or do you take advantage of them because they are saved? Look at your life to evaluate it, and make the necessary changes.

SAY WHAT?
Observation: What do I see?

SO WHAT?
Interpretation: What does it mean?

NOW WHAT?
Application: How does it apply to me?

THEN WHAT?
Implementation: What do I do?

03.20.15 | FRIDAY

1 TIMOTHY 6:3-16

PRIORITIES

SAY WHAT?
What is your goal in life? How does it demonstrate itself?

SO WHAT?
How can you tell if materialism is part of your goal?

NOW WHAT?
How can you keep yourself from pursuing what does not matter?

THEN WHAT?
In light of this passage, what personal commitment can you make?

What is the most important priority in your life? If you could be anything, what would you choose to be? Would you choose to be wealthy and famous, or poor and godly? While most of us might say we would choose to be godly, the reality is that godliness is not the priority of most believers' lives. In this passage, Paul gives Timothy contrasting characteristics between those who choose making money a priority and those who choose godliness as their priority. Those who pursue money may acquire it, but they will also be filled with grief. They will find themselves in ruin and destruction (9-10). They may be very successful, but it will be success in areas that do not matter. Those who pursue godliness will find righteousness, contentment, love, faith, endurance, and gentleness. They may not appear to be successful in the world's eyes, but they are in what really matters. What are you pursuing? What is your goal in life? Is your goal to be successful in what really matters or what doesn't? We can tell by examining which fruits listed are a part of your life. What would God say your priorities are?

XTRA READING
1 TIM 6 (AGAIN)

ONTRACKDEVOTIONS.COM

SATURDAY | 03.21.15

FAN INTO FLAME

2 TIMOTHY 1:1-12

In the book of 2 Timothy, Paul gave challenges to his young spiritual son in the ministry. Paul told Timothy what he must do to be successful in ministry. He began by challenging him to fan into flame his gifts. Did this mean that Timothy had let the flame die? Had Paul not observed him using them at all? Paul probably did not give this challenge because Timothy had let his gifts die. He just wanted Timothy to realize how crucial it would be for him to keep his walk and ministry "white hot" for God. Paul knew that it is easy to let things go for awhile and lose the intensity of the fire that used to be there. He knew that the daily grind is difficult and it is easy to slow down. Paul did not want to see that happen in Timothy's life. Why? - According to verse 7, it is because God did not give us a spirit of timidity but of power, love, and self discipline. In others words, God has given us a spirit that keeps us moving forward and pressing on. Where are you in your walk with God today? Do you need to be reminded to keep fanning the flame in your life and never let it die down, even for a moment? It takes determination, discipline, and God's strength.

SAY WHAT?
Observation: What do I see?

SO WHAT?
Interpretation: What does it mean?

NOW WHAT?
Application: How does it apply to me?

THEN WHAT?
Implementation: What do I do?

03.22.15 | SUNDAY

PROVERBS 24

The book of Proverbs was designed to help us in "attaining wisdom and discipline; in understanding words of insight; in acquiring a disciplined and prudent life, doing what is right and just and fair; in giving prudence to the simple, knowledge and discretion to the young." As you read through this chapter, write down the verses that are most significant to you in your present circumstances.

VERSE	WHAT TRUTH IT COMMUNICATES	HOW IT IMPACTS MY LIFE

ONTRACKDEVOTIONS.COM

MONDAY | 03.23.15

CIVILIAN AFFAIRS

2 TIMOTHY 2:1-13

What was Paul intending to communicate by writing that soldiers do not get involved in civilian affairs? The answer will help us stay the course and prevent us from becoming sidetracked in the ministry God has given us. The first notable phrase in this section is found in verse 4, "no one serving as a soldier." The implication is that we are serving as soldiers and not home on leave, resting. Paul wants us to remember that we are in battle and can't take time off. In light of that, we must not get caught up in "civilian affairs." We are at war and can't be preoccupied by relationships or achievements. We are serving as soldiers. We can't strive for good grades in order to pursue a career that may blind us to the ministry opportunities God gives to us. We are at war, and we must make sure that we do not get involved in things that divert our time, energy, and money from our tasks as soldiers. We must be able to give full attention to our service to God. What "civilian" things have you gotten caught up with? How can you become a soldier again? Remember, we are at war with a fierce enemy. Don't become distracted!

SAY WHAT?
What kind of "civilian affairs" do you struggle with?

SO WHAT?
Why is it difficult to not become entangled in them?

NOW WHAT?
What steps can you take to avoid falling into apathy concerning the war?

THEN WHAT?
In light of this passage, what personal commitment can you make?

XTRA READING
2 TIMOTHY 2

2 TIMOTHY 2:14-26 — WORKMAN

03.24.15 | TUESDAY

SAY WHAT?
Observation: What do I see?

SO WHAT?
Interpretation: What does it mean?

NOW WHAT?
Application: How does it apply to me?

THEN WHAT?
Implementation: What do I do?

What two things did Paul want to be said of Timothy as a workman? Circle them in your Bible. How can we be sure these two things will be said of us? The first characteristic Paul wanted Timothy to be known for was being a workman who did not need to be ashamed. Paul wanted Timothy to live a pure life so that he could hold his head high wherever he went. In order for Timothy to not be ashamed, he had to live a clean life. Are you a workman who is not ashamed? Is your life clean so that you are not ashamed in any place or with anyone? The second characteristic Paul wanted Timothy to be known for was being a workman who correctly handles the Word of Truth. In order for this to be true, he had to read the Word, study it to discover what it is teaching, and memorize it to be able to use it. Knowing God's Word had to be his priority. Are you a workman who can correctly handle the Word of Truth? Do you spend time learning how to use God's Word? In order for you to be known for these characteristics, what changes do you need to make? Is this a priority in your life, or are you satisfied with the way things are?

XTRA READING
2 TIM 2 (AGAIN)

WEDNESDAY | 03.25.15
ENDURE
2 TIMOTHY 3:10-17

So often, when we read our Bibles, we read over phrases that are packed with great meaning and important truth. We can miss the significance of those small phrases. Today, there is a small phrase tucked in the midst of this chapter that could change the way you view the Christian life. Did you notice it? Go back and read verse 12 again. Paul wanted Timothy to understand that he had been asked to endure suffering because of his faith. Paul reminded Timothy of the kinds of persecution he had experienced by the hands of the world. God's deliverance of Paul was to be an encouragement to Timothy to faithfully continue his ministry. Right in the middle of his charge, he said, "everyone who wants to live a godly life...will be persecuted." This means that we, too, will suffer. Be prepared for it. It is a natural part of walking with God. It also means that, if we aren't facing persecution, we may not be living a godly life. How about you? Do you want to live a godly life, even if it means you will face persecution? Although it will come, God will always rescue us. What does your level of persecution reveal?

SAY WHAT?
What kinds of persecution could one face if he were living a godly life?

SO WHAT?
Why do you think those who want to live godly lives face persecution?

NOW WHAT?
What needs to change in your life so that you will become more godly?

THEN WHAT?
In light of this passage, what personal commitment can you make?

XTRA READING
2 TIMOTHY 3

03.26.15 | THURSDAY

2 TIMOTHY 4:9-22

FORGIVENESS

SAY WHAT?
Observation: What do I see?

SO WHAT?
Interpretation: What does it mean?

NOW WHAT?
Application: How does it apply to me?

THEN WHAT?
Implementation: What do I do?

Is it hard for you to forgive people for their mistakes? Do you hold grudges towards people who have hurt you? If you answered yes to either of those questions, you will find encouragement from today's reading. To fully understand this, we must take time to review. In the book of Acts, Paul and Barnabas had taken with them on their missionary journey, a young man named Mark (Acts 12:25). During the trip, Mark became discouraged and left the group to return home. A few years later, Paul and Barnabas were about to embark on another journey. Barnabas wanted to take Mark, but Paul refused. He felt that since Mark had previously failed, they shouldn't give him a second chance. So, Paul took Silas, and Barnabas left with Mark (Acts 15:36-41). We don't hear any more about it until Paul's final comments in today's reading. In verse 11, Paul asked Timothy to bring Mark because he had been helpful to Paul in ministry. Paul had forgiven him and valued his service. He didn't hold a grudge or stubbornly refuse to give him another chance. Do you need to forgive and restore the way Paul did? Could there be steps you need to take today?

XTRA READING
2 TIMOTHY 4

FRIDAY | 03.27.15

ELDER   TITUS 1:5-16

In today's reading, Paul gave Titus a list of requirements for anyone who is being considered for the position of an elder. Why are these requirements important? According to this passage, there are three reasons for this standard. The first reason Paul lists is found in verse 7. These men have been entrusted with God's work. What an elder does is different from any other job a man can have. They are giving God's Word to people. They are involved in teaching it, studying it, using it to correct and rebuke and they have to be credible. Second, we are told in verse 9 that these standards are important because they enable him to encourage others with the truth and refute those who are teaching or living in error. If his life is not what it ought to be, he loses his ability to do this. Third, these standards are vital because there are many rebellious people who teach error and are ruining households. A pastor must be the kind of man who can protect people from the evil intent of these kinds of men. The job of a pastor demands a standard above any other job one might have. Could God be calling you to such a position?

SAY WHAT?
Observation: What do I see?

SO WHAT?
Interpretation: What does it mean?

NOW WHAT?
Application: How does it apply to me?

THEN WHAT?
Implementation: What do I do?

XTRA READING
TITUS 1

03.28.15 | SATURDAY

TITUS 2:1-10
SO THAT

SAY WHAT?
How is the spiritual condition of your youth group/church impacting evangelism in your town?

SO WHAT?
What needs to change to make your group/church more effective in evangelism?

NOW WHAT?
What can you do to see your life and the lives of your friends help others come to know Christ?

THEN WHAT?
In light of this passage, what personal commitment can you make?

If you want to reach the people in your town for Christ, how would you do it? What strategy would be best to see many in your school or workplace trust Christ as their Savior? The most effective evangelism strategy is found in today's reading and, it has been working for over 2,000 years. Did you notice it? Paul told Titus that the most effective way to impact the lost is to have those who are saved growing and walking with God. If you examine each of the "so thats" in today's reading, you see that at the heart of Paul's instruction is evangelism. Paul wanted Titus to teach women the right things so that their lives would not malign the Word of God. Paul wanted Titus to teach young men the right things so that those who opposed them would have nothing to say. Slaves were given instructions on how to live so that their lives would make the teachings about Christ attractive. You see, effective evangelism begins with godly people. If you have a church in which people are walking whole-heartedly with God, then you have a church that can be effective in evangelism. Is your church ready to reach out?

XTRA READING
TITUS 2

SUNDAY | 03.29.15

PROVERBS 25

The book of Proverbs was designed to help us in "attaining wisdom and discipline; in understanding words of insight; in acquiring a disciplined and prudent life, doing what is right and just and fair; in giving prudence to the simple, knowledge and discretion to the young." As you read through this chapter, write down the verses that are most significant to you in your present circumstances.

VERSE	WHAT TRUTH IT COMMUNICATES	HOW IT IMPACTS MY LIFE

03.30.15 | MONDAY

TITUS 3:1-11 — WHAT IS GOOD

SAY WHAT?
Observation: What do I see?

SO WHAT?
Interpretation: What does it mean?

NOW WHAT?
Application: How does it apply to me?

THEN WHAT?
Implementation: What do I do?

In this chapter, we find a wonderful description of salvation. It is a great follow-up to yesterday's reading. You need to be familiar with this section so that when you have an opportunity to share your faith, you can use it. Or, you might need a simple reminder today of what Jesus Christ has done in your life. Paul, in verse 3, describes what we were like before we trusted Christ. Not very flattering, is it? In verse 4-6, he reminds Titus how we have been saved. Our salvation is the work of God in our lives and not something we can do for ourselves. This happened so that we might have the hope of eternal life. And what should our response be to all of this? It should be to devote ourselves to doing good (vs8). Titus needed to stress these truths to people so they would not forget what had happened to them. When you stop to think of what Christ has done for you, how can you do anything but devote yourself to doing good? Reread this section and ask yourself what good you are doing in response to what God has done for you. What impact is your life having on the unsaved. Understanding these truths will change your life and your view of the unsaved.

XTRA READING
TITUS 3

ONTRACKDEVOTIONS.COM

TUESDAY | 03.31.15

FORGIVENESS

PHILEMON 8-22

Philemon is an excellent book on the issue of forgiveness. Paul gave us so much in this short book that will help us learn to forgive others. One of the areas he covers is our responsibility in forgiveness. First, we must be receptive (10-14). We must be willing to open ourselves up to the one who has offended us. If God has done a work in his heart and he seeks forgiveness, we must be open to it. Second, we must be willing to restore him (15-16). If he is truly repentant, we must be willing to not just forgive him, but bring him back to effective ministry and a relationship with us. Third, we must be willing to see restitution take place. It may involve being willing to cancel the debt or allow the person to work off what he owes. We must be willing to allow the wrong to be made right. All of these steps were a part of our salvation the moment we trusted Christ. God was open to our restoration to Him. He allowed us to become His children. He sent Jesus to this earth to pay the price for the debt we owed. Are you willing to do the same? Take the time to also read Matthew 18 to remind yourself of your responsibility to forgive.

SAY WHAT?
Observation: What do I see?

SO WHAT?
Interpretation: What does it mean?

NOW WHAT?
Application: How does it apply to me?

THEN WHAT?
Implementation: What do I do?

XTRA READING
PHILEMON

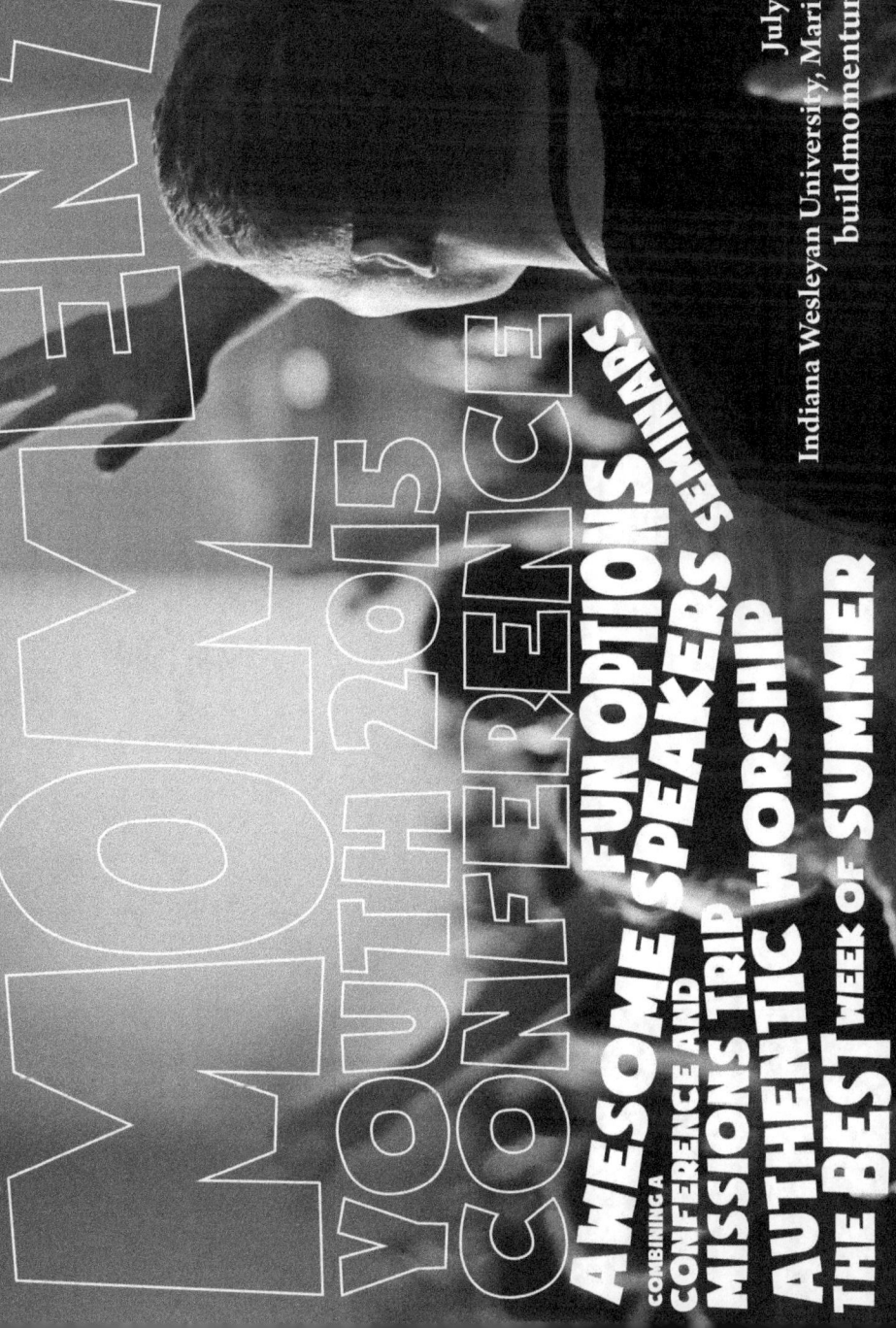

His divine **POWER** has granted to us **ALL THINGS** that pertain to **LIFE AND GODLINESS**, through the knowledge of Him who called us to His own **GLORY** and excellence.

— 2 Peter 1:3

TICKET: ALL-INCLUSIVE

2015
APRIL
1 PETER–JUDE

MONTHLY PRAYER SHEET

"...**The prayer of a righteous man is powerful and effective.**" James 5:16

Reach out to...	How I will do it...	How it went...

Other requests...	Answered	How it was answered...

MONTHLY COMMITMENT SHEET

Name: _____

This sheet is designed to help you make personal commitments each month that will help you grow in your walk with God. Fill it out by determining
1. What will push you
2. What you think you can achieve

If you need help filling out your commitments, seek out someone you trust who can help you. Share your commitments with those who will help keep you accountable to your personal commitment.

Personal Devotions:
How did I do with my commitment last month? _____
I will commit to read the OnTrack Bible passage and devotional thought _____ day(s) each week this month.

Church Attendance:
How did I do last month with my attendance? _____
I will attend Youth/Growth Group _____ time(s) this month.
I will attend the Sunday AM service _____ time(s) this month.
I will attend the Sunday PM service _____ time(s) this month.
I will attend _____ time(s) this month.
I will attend _____ time(s) this month.

Scripture Memory:
How did I do with Scripture memory last month? _____
I will memorize _____ key verse(s) from the daily OnTrack Devotions this month.

Outreach:
How did I do last month at sharing Christ? _____
I will share Christ with _____ person/people this month.
I will serve my local church this month by _____

Other Activities:
List any other opportunities such as events, prayer group, etc., that you will participate in this month. _____

WEDNESDAY | 04.01.15

INHERITANCE   1 PETER 1:1-12

What is the difference between perishing, spoiling, and fading? Is Peter simply saying the same thing in three different ways, or is there more significance to these words? When we look closely at the meaning of these three words, we discover a unique definition for each. First, Peter tells us that our inheritance cannot perish. The definition of perish is that it cannot decay or become corrupt. Secondly, we are told it cannot spoil. The definition of spoil is that it is not affected by evil and it is without defect or flaw. Finally, Peter explains that our inheritance cannot fade, which tells us that time does not affect it. By using these three words, Peter demonstrates that there isn't anything, external or internal, that can or will impact our inheritance. He explains that it is, right now, being kept for us in heaven. How much more certain can your salvation be than for you to know it is waiting in heaven and nothing external or internal can impact it? Who can have this certainty? According to verse 5, those who through faith are shielded by God's power and have trusted Christ as Savior. Allow the certainty of your salvation to give you peace and confidence.

SAY WHAT?
Observation: What do I see?

SO WHAT?
Interpretation: What does it mean?

NOW WHAT?
Application: How does it apply to me?

THEN WHAT?
Implementation: What do I do?

04.02.15 | THURSDAY

1 PETER 1:13-25

BE HOLY

SAY WHAT?
How can you prepare your mind for action?

SO WHAT?
How can you gain more self-control?

NOW WHAT?
What can you do to set your mind on the grace you have been given?

THEN WHAT?
How can you keep from becoming conformed to your evil desires?

How should we respond to the truth revealed to us in yesterday's reading? Should we live in any way we choose since our inheritance is secure? Peter follows his discussion about our salvation with the appropriate response to such incredible truth. First, he tells us that we should prepare our minds for action. We must realize that we are in a spiritual battle and, we must be ready. Secondly, we need to be self-controlled. We must not allow our feelings or desires to control us. Thirdly, we need to set our minds fully on the grace given to us. In other words, we must meditate on what our salvation really means. And finally, we must be sure that we are not conformed to the evil desires we had before we were saved. Why? Because doing so will enable us to be holy, which is our goal. Some might think that because our salvation is secure, we can behave any way we choose. That is not what Scripture teaches. After salvation, we are called to pursue holiness in every aspect of our lives by obeying these four commands. Put numbers next to these four instructions in your Bible to remind you to pursue holiness. It is what God expects.

XTRA READING
1 PETER 1 (AGAIN)

ONTRACKDEVOTIONS.COM

FRIDAY | 04.03.15

A PROCESS

1 PETER 2:1-12

Has a word or phrase from your devotions ever caught your attention and revealed something new from God? There are a few such words in this passage. Did you notice them as you read? The first one is found in verse 5. It is the phrase "being built." Do you realize the significance of those two words? Peter tells us with those words that the Christian life is a process. He wants to emphasize that even though we are saved and our salvation is secure, we are in the "process" of becoming like Christ. When one is born again, God begins the process of making him more like His Son. Peter says that we are "being built" into a spiritual house. We may not be one right now, but each day we get a little closer. It is important to realize that we are in process. Maturity occurs as we grow and move forward in our walk with God. We may not be perfect now, but we ought to see ourselves sinning less, having our devotions more, gaining more boldness, loving people more, etc. We may not be where we want to be, but we are moving toward the goal. Don't become discouraged by the process. Be careful that you don't regress.

SAY WHAT?
Observation: What do I see?

SO WHAT?
Interpretation: What does it mean?

NOW WHAT?
Application: How does it apply to me?

THEN WHAT?
Implementation: What do I do?

XTRA READING
1 PETER 2

04.04.15 | SATURDAY

1 PETER 2:13-25　　　　　　　　　　　　　　　　　　　　**TO THIS...**

SAY WHAT?
In what ways do we respond deceitfully when persecuted?

SO WHAT?
Do we respond by hurling insults at those who persecute us? How?

NOW WHAT?
In what ways do we retaliate?

THEN WHAT?
In light of this passage, what personal commitment can you make?

Have you ever made a decision to do the right thing and then had someone accuse you of doing wrong? How did you feel when you suffered for doing right? If you have ever faced that kind of situation, then today's reading should be helpful. It gives us a sobering, yet encouraging principle regarding unfair treatment. The phrase found in verse 21, "to this you were called" should wake us up a bit. Peter informs us that suffering for doing right is something all Christians should expect and prepare for. Knowing that, we can be encouraged by the fact that Jesus went through the same things. Peter tells us that He did so in order to leave us an example. How close are you to the example He provided? Look at the specifics. There was no deceit found in His mouth. Is there any in yours? He hurled no insults at those who insulted Him. Do you respond this way when people insult you? When He suffered, He made no threats, but instead entrusted Himself to the Father. Sound like you? What a powerful testimony this kind of life would be in our world today! What situation are you facing that demands the imitation of Christ in your life? Are you ready?

XTRA READING
1 PETER 2 (AGAIN)

ONTRACKDEVOTIONS.COM

SUNDAY | 04.05.15

PROVERBS 26

The book of Proverbs was designed to help us in "attaining wisdom and discipline; in understanding words of insight; in acquiring a disciplined and prudent life, doing what is right and just and fair; in giving prudence to the simple, knowledge and discretion to the young." As you read through this chapter, write down the verses that are most significant to you in your present circumstances.

VERSE	WHAT TRUTH IT COMMUNICATES	HOW IT IMPACTS MY LIFE

04.06.15 | MONDAY

1 PETER 3:1-7

INSTEAD

SAY WHAT?
Observation: What do I see?

SO WHAT?
Interpretation: What does it mean?

NOW WHAT?
Application: How does it apply to me?

THEN WHAT?
Implementation: What do I do?

What makes a girl attractive? What should girls strive for? What should guys look for in a girl? In today's reading, Peter gives us an answer. He tells us that while it is fine for girls to braid their hair, wear jewelry and fine clothes, those things should not be where their beauty originates. What ought to make a girl beautiful is what we find on the inside. Her inner self ought to be what she is known for and what makes her attractive. In light of that, girls should be making inner beauty a priority. Much too often, girls spend a lot of time each day working on their outward appearance and very little time making their inner selves beautiful. To God, external beauty has no worth, but a gentle, quiet spirit is of great worth. Guys ought to be looking for girls who have these inner qualities. They are the most important. Outward beauty is not a standard for judging the quality of a person. Both guys and girls need to resist the pressures in today's society to look on the outside and make that the priority. How does your life demonstrate which qualities you value most? How much time do you spend on your inner self?

XTRA READING
1 PETER 3

TUESDAY | 04.07.15

REASONS

1 PETER 3:8-22

What if someone came to you and asked you questions about your faith? Would you be able to give him answers? Could you tell him who Jesus Christ is, and why He came to this earth? What if he wanted to know why you think you are on your way to heaven? What if he wanted to know why you believe the Bible to be the Word of God? Could you tell him? To encourage us along these lines, Peter gives us an admonition in today's passage. In verse 15, he tells us to always be ready to give an answer to everyone who asks us the reason for the hope we have. Specifically, in this context, he explains that these opportunities will come our way as we respond in a godly manner to the suffering we experience for doing what is right. As we respond correctly to our suffering, some may speak maliciously against us, but some will want to know why we have hope in the midst of such hardship. At that moment, we need to be ready to give them the reasons for our hope. Can you verbalize the reasons? In what areas do you need to be better prepared to give an answer? What steps can you take to get yourself ready to give reasons for your hope?

SAY WHAT?
Why have you decided to commit your life to Christ?

SO WHAT?
What reasons would you give for the hope you have in Christ?

NOW WHAT?
What would you say to someone as to why they should trust Christ with their life?

THEN WHAT?
What do I need to do to always be prepared to share this with others?

XTRA READING
1 PETER 3 (AGAIN)

04.08.15 | WEDNESDAY

1 PETER 4:1-11

GIFTS

SAY WHAT?
In what ways has God gifted you?

SO WHAT?
How can you develop them further?

NOW WHAT?
How can you use your gifts to serve the body?

THEN WHAT?
In light of this passage, what personal commitment can you make?

In what ways has God gifted you to serve and encourage the body of Christ? How is the body being influenced by the way you use your gifts? If you do not know the answer to those questions, you cannot comply with what today's passage teaches. In verse 10, we are told to use whatever gifts we have received to serve others. We are to take the gifts God has given to us and use them to encourage and help the body of Christ. In this book, we have already learned that we are called to face all kinds of unjust suffering. While we know it produces positive results in our lives, it does not necessarily make it easier to endure. It is important, therefore, to be a part of the lives of our brothers and sisters by using our gifts to serve them. When we do, we are ministering God's grace in different ways. We don't have the option to sit back and not fulfill our responsibility to the body. If we do, the body loses the grace of God that should be administered. God has a purpose for you and, when you achieve it, you administer God's grace. What role does God want you to play? Do you know what your gifts are? How can you use them? How can you find out and get started?

XTRA READING
1 PETER 4

THURSDAY | 04.09.15

SUFFERING

1 PETER 4:12-19

Does a passage of Scripture like today's reading encourage or discourage you? If you understand the truth involved, it should encourage you. Again, Peter tells us that we will suffer. In fact, in verse 12 he tells us not to be surprised by painful trials as though something strange has happened. What should our response be to this truth? According to verse 13, it is to rejoice. As Christians, we often get bent out of shape when we suffer for doing good. We act as if this is something unheard of and not as Peter warned- something to be expected. Don't acquire or develop a persecution/martyr complex. We ought to rejoice because we are experiencing Christ-like suffering. As a result of suffering for our faith, we will be overjoyed when He appears. If we are being insulted, we view it as a blessing and know that it means the glory of God rests on us. In other words, we should be honored that we are worthy to suffer for being a Christian. Is this your attitude? Have you suffered? How have you responded? Ask God to help you have a right perspective on suffering and a right response to those who cause it.

SAY WHAT?
In what way are you suffering right now for being a Christian?

SO WHAT?
How are you responding to your suffering?

NOW WHAT?
What can you do to respond to suffering like Peter described?

THEN WHAT?
In light of this passage, what personal commitment can you make?

XTRA READING
1 PETER 4 (AGAIN)

04.10.15 | FRIDAY

1 PETER 5:1-11

RESISTING

SAY WHAT?
Observation: What do I see?

SO WHAT?
Interpretation: What does it mean?

NOW WHAT?
Application: How does it apply to me?

THEN WHAT?
Implementation: What do I do?

What does Satan want to see happen in my life? What goals does he have for me? How do I avoid his agenda? How should I respond? The answers to these questions are found in this chapter. They help us avoid his agenda. We need to understand what Satan's goal is for each of us. He is not trying to trip us or cause us to slip a little. His goal is to totally destroy our lives. His agenda is total devastation. He walks around every day, looking for ways to destroy our lives. He will do all he can to bring it to pass. Our response should be to resist him and stand firm. How can we do that? First, we must be faithful to our time in the Word every day. It is our sword and shield against Satan's schemes. We must know what the Word says and how to use it. Knowing what he is trying to do to our lives ought to motivate each of us to never miss a day. Our hearts can be encouraged knowing believers all over the world face the same attacks as we do. God's response is that He will restore us, make us strong, firm, and steadfast. When? After we have suffered "a little while." We can resist Satan, and not allow him to destroy our lives. How can you be better prepared to resist him?

XTRA READING
1 PETER 5

ONTRACKDEVOTIONS.COM

SATURDAY | 04.11.15

ADD...   **2 PETER 1:1-11**

Why should we be motivated to add to our faith the qualities mentioned in verses 5-7? Since we are already on our way to heaven, why put forth the effort? According to verse 8, it is a guard to keep us from becoming ineffective and unproductive. If we do not have those qualities growing in our lives, we will become near-sighted and forget what God has done for us. In verses 3-4, Peter tells us that everything we need for living and for godliness has been given to us. Notice that he says LIFE and godliness. The point is that adding these qualities to our faith does not just impact our "spiritual lives" but impacts everything. God has given us everything we need to be effective and productive in anything we do. Anything we need to live our lives and grow in our faith has been given to us by God and is contained within the pages of Scripture. Since all we need is found in Christ and the knowledge of His Word, we ought to be even more eager to grow in our faith. To neglect your faith results in being ineffective and unproductive in what really matters. How sad to be effective at what does not matter, and ineffective at what does. Which is true of you?

SAY WHAT?
Which of the six items do you need to work on the most? Why?

SO WHAT?
What specific ways can you begin to add them to your life?

NOW WHAT?
How will you tell if they are being added?

THEN WHAT?
In light of this passage, what personal commitment can you make?

XTRA READING
2 PETER 1

04.12.15 | SUNDAY

PROVERBS 27

The book of Proverbs was designed to help us in "attaining wisdom and discipline; in understanding words of insight; in acquiring a disciplined and prudent life, doing what is right and just and fair; in giving prudence to the simple, knowledge and discretion to the young." As you read through this chapter, write down the verses that are most significant to you in your present circumstances.

VERSE	WHAT TRUTH IT COMMUNICATES	HOW IT IMPACTS MY LIFE

MONDAY | 04.13.15

PAY ATTENTION!   2 PETER 1:12-21

Today we see one of the most important statements about the credibility of Scripture. Did you notice it? It is found in verses 20-21. Peter first tells us that he was an eye witness to much of what he had written concerning Christ. One would think that would make him a trustworthy source. However, he tells us that we have an even more trustworthy source than an eyewitness account. What is it? The Bible. Our Bibles are even more certain than someone's eye witness account. The Bible is not simply an account of what an individual has seen, or his interpretation of what he saw. Even though the event was seen in person, the interpretation of what was seen could be biased. How we feel, or what we want to see can alter the accuracy of our account. In contrast, our Bible came to us from men who were guided by the Holy Spirit, so that the words they wrote came not from their memories, but from God Himself. The result is a true, accurate, trustworthy, unbiased account. We can have confidence in every word found in our Bibles. That is why Peter says in verse 19, "you will do well to pay attention to it..." Do you have this kind of confidence?

SAY WHAT?
Observation: What do I see?

SO WHAT?
Interpretation: What does it mean?

NOW WHAT?
Application: How does it apply to me?

THEN WHAT?
Implementation: What do I do?

XTRA READING
2 PETER 1 (AGAIN)

04.14.15 | TUESDAY

2 PETER 2:1-11 | **THEN...**

SAY WHAT?
How will someone who is motivated by personal gain demonstrate his true motive?

SO WHAT?
How will someone, whose true motivation is his love for God and for people, demonstrate those motives?

NOW WHAT?
How can you avoid the trap of a false teacher?

THEN WHAT?
In light of this passage, what personal commitment can you make?

Does today's reading frighten you or give you hope? It can be alarming to realize that there are teachers in this world who are out to lead us astray. It's frightening to realize that someone would introduce false information that purposefully leads us in a wrong direction. They will not speak the truth but, in order to exploit us, will make up stories that sound like the truth. Peter also tells us that their motivation is not to help us, but comes from a desire to get rich. In light of this, what follows is comforting. Verse 9 tells us that God knows how to rescue the godly. Punishment is coming for this kind of teacher. We need to be aware that they are out there and be on guard. We must arm ourselves so that we are not caught by them. We need to examine all teachers and ministers to see if they have true love for us, or if they are using us to become rich. We must study the Bible ourselves to make sure what we believe is truly found in Scripture and does not flow out of someone's personal opinion. God hates false teachers and will punish them. We must arm ourselves, lest we fall prey to their schemes. Daily personal devotions is a good place to start.

XTRA READING
2 PETER 2

WEDNESDAY | 04.15.15

PAY BACK   2 PETER 2:12-22

What can you learn about false teachers in the second half of this chapter? Certainly one other thing is that God has a very grim view of them. Peter gives insights into the characteristics of false teachers. You might want to number them in your Bible. They take good Christian fellowship and use it to practice their ungodliness. They use their positions and abilities to do spiritual work for personal gain. They promise refreshment for people who will follow them and adhere to their teachings, but what they produce in peoples' lives is far from it. They, at one time, have had the appearance of godliness, but the pattern of their lives illustrates that their true nature is far from God. In fact, Peter says that it would have been better for them not to have known the truth, than to have known it and then reject it in order to teach their false doctrine for personal gain. We need to be careful whom we trust and follow. What a blessing to have a teacher who is not like the ones in this chapter! If your teacher is not like this, why not write to thank him? It would encourage him to continue to faithfully walk with God.

SAY WHAT?
Observation: What do I see?

SO WHAT?
Interpretation: What does it mean?

NOW WHAT?
Application: How does it apply to me?

THEN WHAT?
Implementation: What do I do?

XTRA READING
2 PETER 2 (AGAIN)

04.16.15 | THURSDAY

2 PETER 3:1-10
COMING SOON

SAY WHAT?
What can we do to be prepared for Christ's return?

SO WHAT?
In what specific ways can we tell if we really believe He will come back soon?

NOW WHAT?
How are you working to help others be prepared for Christ's return?

THEN WHAT?
In light of this passage, what personal commitment can you make?

Why hasn't Christ returned yet? When will He come again? Does His delay mean He might not ever come? To some, His delay does indicate He is not coming back. However, to the Christian, His return is certain, even though it has not happened yet. Peter closes this book by addressing the scoffers who claim that Christ is not coming back and then explains why Christ's return has been delayed. First, the scoffers who say that things have gone on the same since the beginning of time and, therefore, will continue. Peter tells us that they have not taken into account how God judged the world with the flood, illustrating their point to be false. Peter follows by letting us know that to God a day is like a thousand years. To Him, it has only been about 2 days since Jesus left the earth. Peter closes by telling us the return of Jesus Christ has been delayed to provide more people with the opportunity to be saved. His delay is not the neglect of His promise, but the fulfillment of His promise. When His patience has ended, He will come. Are you ready? Who can you tell that the return of Christ has been delayed to provide him an opportunity for salvation?

XTRA READING
2 PETER 3

FRIDAY | 04.17.15

SO THEN...

2 PETER 3:11-18

What does the truth of yesterday's reading mean to us who are alive today? How should we act since the return of Christ is certain? Peter answers these questions as he closes this book. First, he tells us that we should live holy and godly lives (vs11). The knowledge that the return of Christ is certain, yet delayed in order for the last ones to be saved, should motivate us to live lives that show the difference Jesus Christ makes. Secondly, we should make every effort to be found spotless, blameless, and at peace with God (vs14). All of our energy should be spent becoming a person who could be described this way. Again, Peter reminds us that the delay is so that others can be saved. Our light in the darkness is vital in order for them to see their need for Christ. Thirdly, Peter tells us to be on our guard. There are forces at work designed to teach us error and make us insecure in our relationship with Christ. Both of these could make us ineffective in reaching our worlds for Christ. We must help others see and then take advantage of their opportunities to trust Christ. In light of Christ's return, we must live godly lives. Are you doing that?

SAY WHAT?
Observation: What do I see?

SO WHAT?
Interpretation: What does it mean?

NOW WHAT?
Application: How does it apply to me?

THEN WHAT?
Implementation: What do I do?

XTRA READING
2 PETER 3 (AGAIN)

04.18.15 | SATURDAY

1 JOHN 1:5-10 — CLEANSING

SAY WHAT?
For what sin do you need to seek God's forgiveness?

SO WHAT?
From what sin in your past have you sought God's forgiveness, but not His cleansing?

NOW WHAT?
How can you apply what you have read today to these two areas?

THEN WHAT?
In light of this passage, what personal commitment can you make?

If 1 John 1:9 were not in the Bible, what would we miss? What kind of impact would it have on our lives if God had left it out? We would miss one of the foundational truths in all the Scriptures. John tells us that God can do something to relieve the burden and guilt of sin. We all violate His standard, and feel guilty about it. How comforting to know that we can go to God, confess it, and He will forgive us. What hope this verse gives! However, the truth does not stop there. John tells us not only can we find forgiveness, but He will "purify us from all unrighteousness." It is one thing to be forgiven; it is something more to be cleansed. The guilt can be taken away because we have experienced His forgiveness and have been cleansed. We do not have to keep repeating it and continually seek God's forgiveness. What sin in your life do you need to confess and seek forgiveness from God? From what sin in your life do you need to be cleansed? You do not have to live under the burden of guilt. Do not allow Satan to neutralize you with your past sin. Go to God and allow His forgiveness and cleansing to give you peace and hope.

XTRA READING
1 JOHN 1

SUNDAY | 04.19.15

PROVERBS 28

The book of Proverbs was designed to help us in "attaining wisdom and discipline; in understanding words of insight; in acquiring a disciplined and prudent life, doing what is right and just and fair; in giving prudence to the simple, knowledge and discretion to the young." As you read through this chapter, write down the verses that are most significant to you in your present circumstances.

VERSE | WHAT TRUTH IT COMMUNICATES | HOW IT IMPACTS MY LIFE

04.20.15 | MONDAY

1 JOHN 2:1-14

EVIDENCE

SAY WHAT?
Observation: What do I see?

SO WHAT?
Interpretation: What does it mean?

NOW WHAT?
Application: How does it apply to me?

THEN WHAT?
Implementation: What do I do?

How can you tell if an individual is a believer? What characteristics demonstrate that he is truly saved? The book of 1 John is filled with characteristics that show up in the lives of those who have eternal life. As you read through this book, make a note in your Bible of what they are. Put a - next to those which are signs of unbelief and a + next to those that are true of one who is saved. In today's reading, we find three characteristics of those who are saved. John wrote in verse 3 that if we are truly saved we will obey the commands of God. If we say we are saved, but do not obey what Scripture teaches, we are liars. In verse 6, we read that we who are truly saved will walk as Jesus did. There will be evidence that we are becoming more like Christ in every area of our lives. We see in verse 9, that our behavior towards our brothers in Christ also demonstrates our standing before God. We who are saved will love our brothers. Those who are not will hate their brothers. How does your life measure up to these three standards? Do they give you assurance of your salvation or cause you to doubt the sincerity of it?

XTRA READING
1 JOHN 2

TUESDAY | 04.21.15

WORLD   1 JOHN 2:15-29

What does John mean when he tells us not to love the world? Does it mean that we cannot be really close to anyone who is unsaved? The Greek word for world in this verse is cosmos. It is a word that refers to the world's system, not to the people who live in it. It is the system that exists in our world that is opposed to God. John wanted us to know that we should not love what the world encourages us to love. Someone who loves the world is someone who finds pleasure in what the world offers. He is someone who wants the same lifestyle and value system that he sees on TV. It is wishing he could be like the people around him who are not obedient to God and wanting to engage in their activities. The reason is found in verse 16. John tells us that the world is made up of the desires of our fallen, sinful nature and, the temptations that face us encourage us to violate God's standard. It also includes boasting about what we have as though it came from our human efforts, not God's. How do you feel about the world and its system? Do you envy it and let it entice you, or does your heart become burdened as you see the lives it destroys? What does your response tell you?

SAY WHAT?
What are some examples of things in the world that are easy for us to love?

SO WHAT?
How does someone demonstrate they love the things of the world?

NOW WHAT?
How can you protect yourself from developing a love for the world?

THEN WHAT?
In light of this passage, what personal commitment can you make?

XTRA READING
1 JOHN 2 (AGAIN)

04.22.15 | WEDNESDAY

1 JOHN 3:1-10

VICTORY

SAY WHAT?
Observation: What do I see?

SO WHAT?
Interpretation: What does it mean?

NOW WHAT?
Application: How does it apply to me?

THEN WHAT?
Implementation: What do I do?

Was John's intent in these verses to communicate to us that any sin we commit indicates that we are not really saved? Some would say that is exactly what this verse teaches. A closer look, however, reveals a different interpretation. John, in this section, was again emphasizing that those who are really saved will demonstrate it by their behavior. In verse 3, he said that anyone who is saved purifies himself. He works hard to get rid of sin in his life, and his desire is to be pure in all areas. Jesus Christ came into this world to take away our sin. After salvation, we begin to realize what sin is, what it does, and we hate it. We do not want it to be part of our lives. Our desire is to purify ourselves from sin. The point John is making is not that people who are saved never sin, but that people who are saved do not "keep on sinning." That means that sin is not the pattern of their lives. They do not continue to live a life of sin, but strive to live a life of purity. How I respond to sin indicates whether my salvation is genuine or not. What pattern do you see in your life? Do you see yourself gaining victory over more areas of sin?

XTRA READING
1 JOHN 3

THURSDAY | 04.23.15

DO SOMETHING

1 JOHN 3:11-24

How do you feel when you see someone in your youth group or church who has a material need? What do you do when you hear he has no money to pay for basic needs or simple wants? How do you respond to the difficult circumstances in the lives of others when you hear about them? The response you give in these circumstances will reveal something about where you stand before God. John tells us that turning a blind eye to obvious needs demonstrates that we do not have God's love in us. In other words, it shows we are not saved. It is not enough to see the needs and communicate them to others; it is a demonstration of love when we do something to meet the needs. He tells us not to be the kind of people who see needs and do nothing about them. In fact, when we see needs and do something to meet them, we demonstrate that we are saved. It is good to be burdened about needs; it is better to do something about them. When is the last time you did something about a need you knew about? Are you aware of someone who has a need with which you can help? Do not love with words only; love with actions! Look around today and see what needs you can meet.

SAY WHAT?
What needs are you currently aware of?

SO WHAT?
In what ways can you help with those needs besides praying about them?

NOW WHAT?
How can you become more sensitive to meeting the needs of others?

THEN WHAT?
In light of this passage, what personal commitment can you make?

XTRA READING
1 JOHN 3 (AGAIN)

04.24.15 | FRIDAY

1 JOHN 4:7-21

BROTHERLY LOVE

SAY WHAT?
Observation: What do I see?

SO WHAT?
Interpretation: What does it mean?

NOW WHAT?
Application: How does it apply to me?

THEN WHAT?
Implementation: What do I do?

When John wrote this book, what main ideas do you think he wanted to communicate? As you read today's passage did you conclude that one of the points he was making was that we all need to love our brothers? That is one of the primary themes mentioned over and over throughout this book. Why was it so important to John? He wanted to ensure that we know what our love for each other says to the world. Jesus told the disciples that the world would be able to tell they were disciples by their love for each other (John 13:35). In fact, in that passage, He told them they were to love each other as He had loved them. The same level of compassion that Christ has shown to us is what we are to show our brothers. With the same selflessness Christ demonstrated, we are to seek to meet the needs of our brothers. The one thing that ought to show the world that we are disciples of Christ is the love we express to others. When people spend time with us, they should notice our love for each other. Using that measuring stick, how are you doing? Can people see you are a disciple, based on your love for the all the people in your world?

XTRA READING
1 JOHN 4

SATURDAY | 04.25.15

THESE THREE
1 JOHN 5:1-12

What does John mean by saying that we have three witnesses that Jesus Christ is God - the Spirit, water, and the blood? There is some debate about this passage, but its truth is crucial and very clear. There are some who would argue that Jesus Christ was not God, but simply a man. Others would at least say that God came upon the man Jesus Christ when He was baptized. In other words, he became God. However, this passages makes it clear that those positions are not true. John tells us that both Jesus' baptism (water), and His crucifixion (blood), prove that He was God. When referring to the water and blood, John used the verb "came by." He uses that verb to emphasize that Jesus Christ wasn't made God by these things but, as God, came by these things. John explained that His earthly ministry proved He was God- from His birth to His baptism to His crucifixion. Beyond these two, the Holy Spirit also testifies to us that He is God! We can have confidence that Jesus Christ IS God. His baptism, His crucifixion, and the Holy Spirit demonstrate it. What people do you know who would be open to this message?

SAY WHAT?
Observation: What do I see?

SO WHAT?
Interpretation: What does it mean?

NOW WHAT?
Application: How does it apply to me?

THEN WHAT?
Implementation: What do I do?

XTRA READING
1 JOHN 5

04.26.15 | SUNDAY

PROVERBS 29

The book of Proverbs was designed to help us in "attaining wisdom and discipline; in understanding words of insight; in acquiring a disciplined and prudent life, doing what is right and just and fair; in giving prudence to the simple, knowledge and discretion to the young." As you read through this chapter, write down the verses that are most significant to you in your present circumstances.

VERSE	WHAT TRUTH IT COMMUNICATES	HOW IT IMPACTS MY LIFE

MONDAY | 04.27.15

EVALUATION

1 JOHN 5:13-21

We have just completed reading through this great book. Throughout I John, we find characteristics of those who know Jesus Christ as their personal Savior. John closes this book by stating that it was written so that you might know you have eternal life. As you have read through it, do you see evidence that you are saved? Use today's questions to help you evaluate what you have learned. John wants you to know you have eternal life. Be honest about what you discover, and be sure to talk to someone who can help you understand what you have discovered about yourself, as well as how to respond to it.

SAY WHAT?

List some of the characteristics found in this book of those who are saved.

SO WHAT?

List some of the characteristics John gave in this book for those who are not saved.

NOW WHAT?

Summarize what your answers to these two questions tell you about where you stand in your relationship to God.

XTRA READING
1 JOHN 5 (AGAIN)

2 JOHN 4-11 — DEMONSTRATED LOVE

04.28.15 | TUESDAY

SAY WHAT?
Observation: What do I see?

SO WHAT?
Interpretation: What does it mean?

NOW WHAT?
Application: How does it apply to me?

THEN WHAT?
Implementation: What do I do?

Can one say that he loves God and is a Christian, but not obey what the Bible teaches? No, he cannot, according to today's reading. John wrote to some friends here in this small book and gave them a command. The command was to love one another. What does it mean to walk in love? According to these verses, it means to live a life of obedience. It requires loving Christ so much that you want to do what He says. It requires that you deliberately seek obedience. It requires obedience by choice, not by obligation or duty. All of this implies firsthand knowledge of His Word. We show our love by our desire to know what God's Word teaches and then by living in obedience to what it tells us to do. We cannot say we truly love God if we do not do what He says. What does your life tell you about how much you love God? Are you obedient to His Word? Do you read it and study it so that you know what He expects of you? In what way can you be obedient today in order to show God and those who observe your life that you love Him? Find a new way to show Him how much you love Him. It is the least you can do.

XTRA READING: 2 JOHN

WEDNESDAY | 04.29.15

SOURCE OF JOY

3 JOHN 1-8

What brings you the most joy in your life? As you think back over this past week, what event brought a smile to your face? What is it about you that gives other people joy? In today's reading, we get a glimpse into the heart of John and learn how he would answer those questions and, how we can be an encouragement to others. John says that what brings him the most joy is to know that his children, those on whom he has had a spiritual impact, are walking in the truth. His joy comes from how those to whom he had ministered were continuing in their faith. He was concerned about their spiritual well-being even as they grew older. Even more amazing to consider is the potential that they had to be either a source of great joy or great sorrow to John. He loved them and cared about their walks with God. We sometimes forget the impact our lives have on those who, in the past, have invested time in us. We do not consider the pain or hurt we inflict when we do not walk with God. How much joy do those who have invested time and effort into your life get as they observe your walk of faith? Have you ever thanked them for their efforts? Why not do so today?

SAY WHAT?
Write down the names of people who have invested in your life?

SO WHAT?
How would you guess your walk with God is impacting them?

NOW WHAT?
What can you change in your life in order to bring more joy to them?

THEN WHAT?
In light of this passage, what personal commitment should you make?

04.30.15 | THURSDAY

JUDE 17-23

BUT YOU...

SAY WHAT?
Observation: What do I see?

SO WHAT?
Interpretation: What does it mean?

NOW WHAT?
Application: How does it apply to me?

THEN WHAT?
Implementation: What do I do?

What should we do, knowing that people will come who want to destroy us and our faith? The answer is found in today's reading. Did you notice it? This book informs those who read it that there will be people whose sole purpose is to destroy the message of the Gospel. In light of that, we are told by Jude to contend for the Gospel so that it remains pure. He ends the book by giving us two things we can do to prepare ourselves for their attacks. First, we need to build ourselves up in the faith (vs20). In order to do this, we must study our Bibles and make sure we know what it teaches. We must be continually growing and learning more. Second, we should pray in the Holy Spirit (vs20). He alone, not our selfishness or intellect, needs to be guiding our prayers. The bottom line is that we need to be committed to personal study and prayer. These two will give us the knowledge and the strength to be able to recognize and fight off the false teaching that will come. What are you doing to prepare yourself to be able to contend for the faith? Is your devotional life consistent? Daily? Do you pray guided by the Holy Spirit? How can you be more effective in those areas?

XTRA READING
JUDE

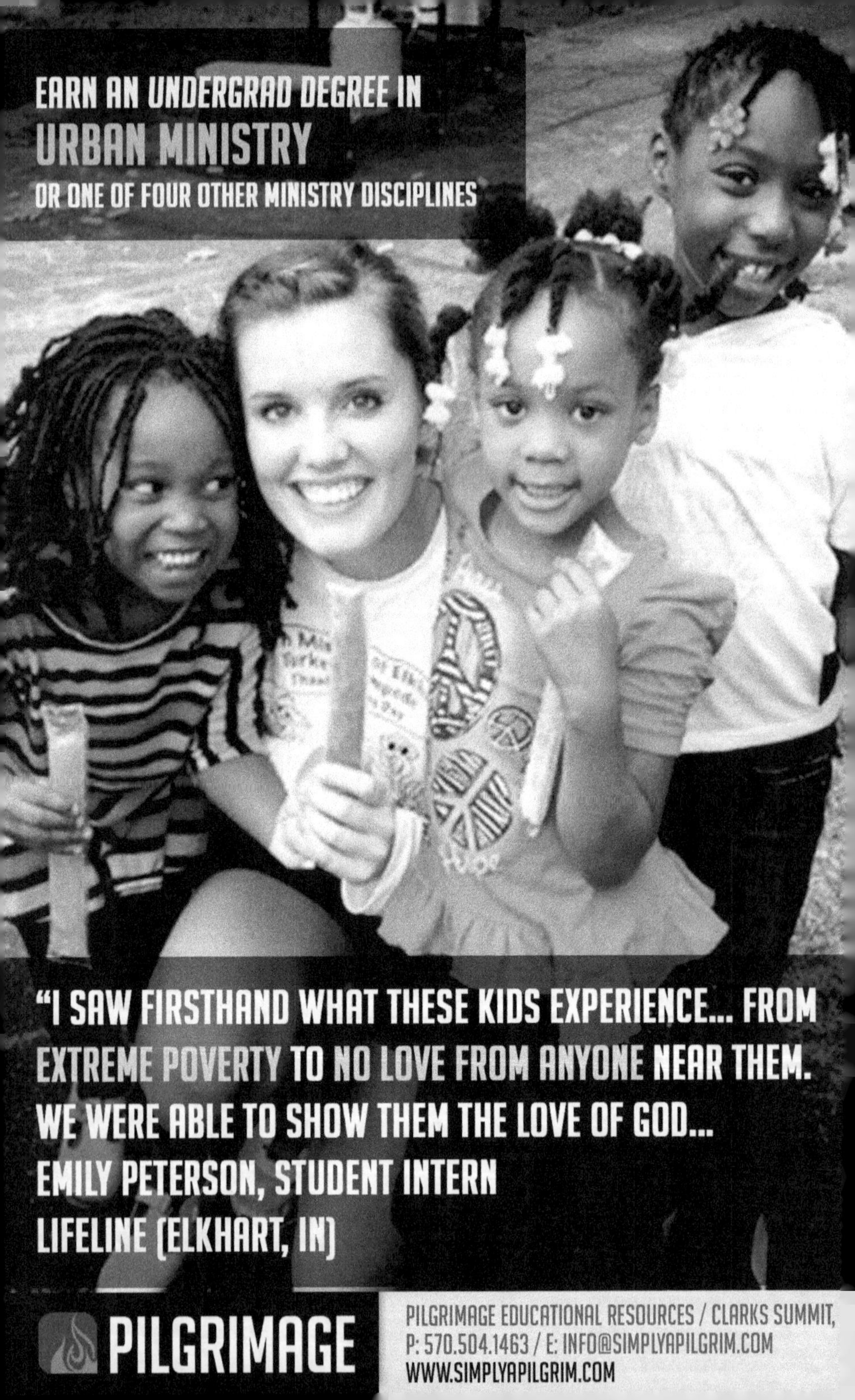

TEEN LEADERSHIP CONFERENCE
JULY 20-25 • JULY 27-AUGUST 1

GROW

MORE INFO AND REGISTRATION ONLINE AT BBC.EDU/TLC

EARLY BIRD DISCOUNTS AVAILABLE!

2015 FOCUS

This year at TLC, we will focus on how we can make sure that above all else we are GROWING spiritually. From personal examination and confession, to personal growth and development, the week will be designed to help us gain a better understanding of what growth looks like and how to make it a reality in our lives.

TLC is hosted by Baptist Bible College in Clarks Summit, PA. Join students and youth workers from across the country for a week of true life change!

www.ingramcontent.com/pod-product-compliance
Lightning Source LLC
Chambersburg PA
CBHW052308300426
44110CB00035B/2179